Hello, Is There Any Body There?

A farce
Ian Hornby

New Theatre Publications - London
www.plays4theatre.com

The edition published in 2013

New Theatre Publications

2 Hereford Close | Warrington | Cheshire | WA1 4HR | 01925 485605

www.plays4theatre.com   email: info@plays4theatre.com

New Theatre Publications is the trading name of the publishing house that is owned by members of the Playwrights' Co-operative. This innovative project was launched on the 1st October 1997 by writers Paul Beard and Ian Hornby with the aim of encouraging the writing and promotion of the very best in New Theatre by Professional and Amateur writers for the Professional and Amateur Theatre at home and abroad.

ISBN 9 781 840 94000 8

Characters
Lady Amelia, an authoress
Sir Malcolm, Amelia's husband
Freddy Lyons, a family friend
Mabel, the maid
Dianne Sides, a Police Inspector
Vic/DC Fickey
WPC Nunnall, glamorous WPC
Smalls, the butler
Miss Marbles, a famous detective novelist

Synopsis of scenes
ACT I - early evening, shortly after dinner
ACT II – later the same day
ACT III – later the same day

Performing Licence Applications

A performing licence for these plays will be issued by "New Theatre Publications" subject to the following conditions.

Conditions

1. That the performance fee is paid in full on the date of application for a licence.

2. That the name of the author(s) is/are clearly shown in any programme or publicity material.

3. That the author(s) is/are entitled to receive two complimentary tickets to see his/her/their work in performance if they so wish.

4. That a copy of the play is purchased from New Theatre Publications for each named speaking part and a minimum of three copies purchased for backstage use.

5. That a copy of any review be forwarded to New Theatre Publications.

6. That the New Theatre Publications logo is clearly shown on any publicity material. This is available on our website.

Fees

Details of script prices and fees payable for each performance or public reading can be obtained by telephone to (+44) 01925 485605 or to the address below.

Alternatively, latest prices can be obtained from our website www.plays4theatre.com where credit/debit cards can be used for payment.

To apply for a performing licence for any play please write to New Theatre Publications 2 Hereford Close, Warrington, Cheshire WA1 4HR or email info@plays4theatre.com with the following details:-

1. Name and address of theatre company.

2. Details of venue including seating capacity.

3. Dates of proposed performance or public reading.

4. Contact telephone number for Author's complimentary tickets.

Or apply directly via our website at www.plays4theatre.com

Hello... is There Any Body There?
A Farce by Ian Hornby
For more plays by Ian Hornby see www.scripts4theatre.com

CAST *(in order of appearance)*

Lady Amelia Simpson-Squire. . . . . *an authoress*
Sir Malcolm Squire. . . . . *Amelia's husband*
Freddy Lyons. . . . . *a family friend*
Mabel. . . . . *the maid*
Dianne Sides. . . . . *a Police Inspector*
Vic/DC Fickey
WPC Nunnall. . . . . *a glamorous WPC*
Smalls. . . . . *the butler*
Miss Marbles. . . . . *a famous detective novelist*

The play is set in the lounge of the country seat of Sir Malcolm Squire and Lady Amelia Simpson-Squire. The lounge is expensively furnished in the manner of a country manor, and is situated in an isolated position on the moors.

ACT I

It is early evening, shortly after dinner. Sir Malcolm is snoring in the armchair R, an almost-empty brandy glass hanging from his right hand and a copy of "The Times" on his lap open at the crossword. Lady Amelia is sitting of the settee L writing notes in a jotter on her lap. She is eating chocolates from a large chocolate box by her side.

Shortly after the curtain rises, Lady Amelia looks up and notices the audience.

Amelia   *(peers out at the audience)* Oh, hello. I didn't see you there. Welcome to Squire Grange. My name is Amelia... Lady Amelia Simpson-hyphen-Squire, to be precise, and I'm a writer of mystery novels. In case you haven't gathered yet, this play is a murder mystery. And it's *terribly* serious, so no giggling at the back.

        (Indicates Malcolm.) That vision of loveliness is my beloved husband Sir Malcolm. *(Holds up her hand as if for silence.)* No, don't say it, I know what you're thinking. But he hasn't been murdered. Not yet, anyway. He's always like that after dinner. Inside that strange looking sack of potatoes lies the man I married all those years ago. *Very deep* inside.

        (Malcolm gives a particularly loud snore.) Sir Malcolm used to be a stockbroker - an appropriate name, stockbroker - all the people who bought his stock went broke

- but he doesn't work any more. He prefers to live the life of a country squire on the proceeds of *my* novels.

Anyway, back to the plot. As you've probably gathered by now *somebody* is going to be done away with. I shan't tell you who, because that would ruin the plot. And anyway, to tell you the absolute truth, I'm not exactly sure myself who it'll be... Even though I'm the star of this play they haven't told me either. Confused? Yes, me too. Still, I'm sure we'll find out before too long.

(The doorbell rings off R.)

Oh, you'll have to excuse me. It seems we have company.

(Smalls enters R followed by Freddy. Smalls wears his butler's uniform of white shirt and black tie and trousers. Freddy is gentle, old-fashioned and soft-spoken. He wears a tweed overcoat and hat over a sports jacket, casual shirt and tweed trousers.)

Smalls	*(announcing)* Mr Lyons, Ma'am.
Amelia	Thank you, Smalls. Hello, Freddy. Have a good trip?

(Smalls exits L.)

Freddy	*(moves L)* 'Evening, Amelia. Yes, not bad, really. The M25 was a bit crowded, but after that it was plain sailing all the way.

(Freddy moves over to Malcolm, leans towards him and looks at him curiously. Malcolm gives another loud snore and Freddy is startled.)

Freddy	Malcolm er... *in*, is he?
Amelia	I'm not sure. His body's been there for the past hour or so, but as for his mind...? Why don't you give him a knock?

(Freddy is about to knock on Malcolm's head, then decides better of it.)

Freddy	*(stands upright)* No, I'd better not. Last time I tried that he accused me of stealing his brandy.
Amelia	And you're still alive to tell the tale?
Freddy	*(ignores her joke; moves towards the sofa)* And how's Amelia?
Amelia	*(with a sigh)* Oh, I'm O.K... A little bored, perhaps, but O.K. all the same.
Freddy	*(moves down)* Bored!? How can you say you're bored out here? Lovely house like this, servants to do all the work... and that view. *(Indicates through a fourth wall "window" towards the audience)* I never get tired of looking out across those moors... it's so peaceful. You should count your

blessings, Amelia…

Amelia But that's exactly *why* I'm so bored, Freddy. I *know* it's lovely out here, but nothing ever happens. I live the life of an old country dowager… I'd like a bit of excitement every now and again. After all, Freddy, I'm only forty… *(Corrects herself quickly)* thirty-five.

Freddy I never realised you felt that way, old girl. You've always seemed so happy here.

Amelia Oh, don't get me wrong - I don't mean to complain. I *was* very happy here… when the children were at home. But now they've flown the nest…

Freddy Well, as you said, you're still young. Why don't you have another…?

Malcolm *(awakes and holds out his glass)* Don't mind if I do, old boy. Brandy, thanks.

Freddy *(sarcastic)* Ah, Milord awakes. Hard day at the office, Malcolm?

Malcolm Now don't you start, Freddy. I get enough flak from Amelia about my lack of er… activity. You'd never know I was the star of this play. *(Imitates Amelia)* "You need more exercise, Malcolm", "You should take up jogging, Malcolm"… "You should go on a diet, Malcolm"…

Amelia It's for your own good, my darling. You're too sedentary. You make a hibernating tortoise look hyperactive. The only exercise you ever take is lifting a brandy glass. You could captain England for that. It's not healthy… you'll kill yourself.

Malcolm I'll have you know that brandy is very good for you - in moderation, of course.

Amelia In moderation!

Malcolm Don't know what *you're* worried about, anyway old thing… I'm fully insured, you know. If I were to pop off tomorrow you'd be rolling in it.

Amelia *(not listening; consults her jotter)* Now you've given me an idea. What if I was to slip something lethal into your brandy? Nobody would ever know. Old Doc Jones would have enough trouble finding your body, let alone the poison.

Malcolm No use, Amelia. One of those pathologist chappies'd be bound to find it in my bloodstream.

Amelia They'd have enough trouble finding the blood in *your* bloodstream. It'll be easy when you pop off - you're half - embalmed *already*!

Freddy I say, you two… Steady on, will you? This is getting a bit

	morbid, isn't it? All this talk of killing and popping off?
Malcolm	Don't worry about us, Freddy! We often sit and chat like this. We devise horrible plans for each other's grisly deaths, trying to invent the perfect crime.
Freddy	Ugh! How disgusting. Why on earth…?
Malcolm	Where d'you think Amelia gets all the plots for her novels?
Freddy	Oh, I see.. You mean…?
Malcolm	D'you recall "The Paddington Murders"?
Freddy	Ah, yes… one of your best, Amelia.
Amelia	Thank you, Freddy. Flattery will get you everywhere.
Malcolm	Well, d'you remember Major Fotheringay…? The one who was found beaten to death with a British Rail pork pie?
Freddy	Yes.
Malcolm	*(proudly)* That was me.
Amelia	And the maid who was strangled in the tunnel..? Yours truly.
Freddy	How gruesome! I don't think I should be able to sleep at night if my wife and I talked like that… if I was married, that is.
Malcolm	*(to Amelia; conspiratorially)* Now there's a thought, Amelia. Freddy's not married… He'd be the *perfect* victim. Nobody's expecting him home.
Amelia	That's true. *(Teasing)* Er… Freddy… Did you…er… *tell* anyone where you were going this weekend?
Freddy	*(feels his collar; uneasy)* What…? Well, er… *(Gulp)* My doctor, er… No… Er… The milkman… *(Pulls himself together)* Now look, you two, you're making me nervous. It's not natural, the way you're carrying on.
Amelia	Oh, I don't know. It does add a bit of spice to our otherwise dull existence. Keeps us on our toes, as it were. After all, there's precious little else to do round here *but* talk.
Freddy	Yes, but even so…
Amelia	Don't worry, Freddy… if Malcolm really wanted to see me off, all he'd need to do would be to creep up behind me one day and say "Boo!" It's so quiet around here the shock'd kill me outright.
Freddy	I still say it's not natural.
Amelia	Natural or not, Freddy, we have to come up with an idea soon. The deadline, if you'll pardon the expression, for this book is in five weeks, and so far all the plots we've managed to come up with have already been done.
Freddy	You know I've often wondered about that. When you do come up with an idea, how do you check whether somebody's used

	it before? What would happen if you unwittingly wrote the same plot as Agatha Christie, for example?
Amelia	I'd be in breach of copyright if it was exactly the same. If it wasn't *quite* the same but close enough the public wouldn't bother to buy the book.
Freddy	So how *do* you check?
Amelia	We read a lot. We get copies of pretty well every murder mystery that's published. I read a lot of legal reports and so on. I pride myself on being somewhat of an expert on murders. If I *did* want to murder Malcolm, I've so many ideas stored away up here, *(indicates her head)* it'd take a *very* clever policeman to solve it.
Freddy	*(thoughtful)* Yes… I suppose so.
Amelia	And that's part of my problem. Every new idea I think of gets sort of… sidetracked onto a plot that's been done before. I could do with making my mind a complete blank. You know… a bit like Malcolm's.
Malcolm	Thank you, Amelia.
Amelia	You're welcome, my love.
Freddy	Why don't you try a hypnotist? They're supposed to be able to make your mind a blank.
Amelia	No, thank you. There's quite enough sinister goings on in my mind without someone else stirring up the murky depths. I just wish I could borrow someone else's mind for a few days… a clean, unsullied one who could look at the problem from a fresh viewpoint.
Malcolm	Tell you what, Amelia… let's tap Freddy's brain. He's fairly unsullied. Maybe he'll come up with some fresh ideas.
Amelia	Yes, that's a good idea!
Freddy	Oh no, now wait a minute…
Amelia	Oh, go on, Freddy. It'd be ever such a help.
Malcolm	Come on, Freddy, let the darker side of your imagination run free.
Amelia	We'll have to give him a clue, darling. He's never murdered anyone before…, *(Teasing)* have you, Freddy?
Freddy	What…!? Well, I er… No! Of course not! And I'm not about to start…
Malcolm	*(to Freddy; deep in thought)* Now, let's see… Just suppose you and Amelia were… er… having an affaire behind my back.
Freddy	*(shocked)* What!? But Malcolm, you know me. I'm your best

friend… I wouldn't… How could you suggest I would do such a thing? With Amelia of all people!

Amelia   *(feigns hurt)* Oh, woe! To have come to this! The Flower Festival Queen of 1966, Deb of the Decade, Bride of the Month, Lady of the Manor… and now… spurned! Not only by my husband, but also by the man of my dreams…

Malcolm   Shut up, Amelia. This isn't Withering Depths, you know.

Amelia   Sorry, dear. Just thought I'd add a bit of culture. Carry on waffl… with your ideas, my darling.

Malcolm   Now, Freddy… I've already said Amelia'd be worth a fortune if I were to suddenly pop off, so it'd be well worth your while. Now how would you go about it?

Freddy   No! You can stop this right now! I *refuse* to take part in your morbid little games.

Amelia   Oh, don't be such a stuffed shirt, Freddy. It's only a bit of fun.

Freddy   *(weakens)* You have a strange idea of fun…

Malcolm   Yes, come on, Freddy. Don't be a spoilsport.

Amelia   It'd be a change from "Trivial Pursuit" and "Monopoly".

Freddy   *(undecided)* Yes, that's true. Well, alright then… But reluctantly, mind you.

Malcolm   Good show, old man.

    (Malcolm and Amelia sit forward in their seats waiting eagerly for Freddy to start. Amelia has her jotter at the ready. Freddy remains pensive.)

Amelia   *(after a few moments wait)* In your own time, Freddy.

    (Freddy remains deep in thought. Amelia and Malcolm look at each other impatiently. Amelia starts to drum her fingers on her jotter impatiently. Malcolm looks at his watch.)

Malcolm   By "in your own time" Amelia meant *before* we die of old age, Freddy.

Freddy   Alright, alright, don't rush me. It's just that I… I don't know where to start. I've never even dreamed of such things.

Amelia   Splendid! Then nobody would suspect you. You're applying your fresh and unsullied mind to it, so perhaps you *can* invent the perfect crime. *(After a pause)* If you do, Freddy, you *will* let me use it to murder someone, won't you? In my book., I mean.

Freddy   Oh, yes, of course you can. I'm hardly going to use it myself, am I? I know I'm the star of this play, but I *still* think I'm hardly the stuff that perfect murders come from.

Amelia   But surely you must have considered it, just once in your life.

Hasn't anyone ever got you so mad that you considered, just for a split second...

Freddy   Certainly not! I'm a pacifist, a wimp.

Malcolm   Yes, we know that old man, but you never know. Go on... It won't hurt to give it a try. *(In a sinister voice)* Give free rein to your darker side.

Freddy   Well, alright, if you insist... I'll try.

Malcolm   Good show. We're all ears.

(Freddy starts to think and Amelia and Malcolm move forwards on their seats again ready to listen.)

Freddy   Now... let's see. For the perfect crime it needs to be undetectable. It would have to be something natural, something involving your everyday activities...

Amelia   No use going down that path, Freddy. Malcolm hasn't *got* any activities, unless, of course, you could get him to have a heart attack from over-exerting his brandy glass. *(Her mind wandering)* I wonder if anyone's ever died from inactivity? You know... just sort of run down and stopped altogether... Like a car first thing on a cold morning if you put the choke in too soon.

Malcolm   Amelia! If you don't keep quiet, I'll choke *you*! This is Freddy's murder, not yours. *(To Freddy)* She never stops, Freddy. She's like an over-inflated bag of wind.

Amelia   Now *there's* an idea... poisoned baked beans...

Malcolm   Amelia!

Amelia   Sorry, Malcolm. Consider me thoroughly chastised. Sorry, Freddy, carry on.

Freddy   It would have to be something normal so as not to arouse suspicion. What do you do each day? Have you a routine?

Malcolm   Well, now, let's see... I usually wake up about nine and have my early morning cup of...

Amelia   *(interrupts)* Brandy.

Malcolm   ...Coffee. *(Gives Amelia a disapproving look.)* Then I read "The Times" for half an hour or so. Then I get out of bed, go to the bathroom...

Amelia   Ever seen anybody clean his teeth using Napoleon Four Star as a mouthwash, Freddy?

Malcolm   Amelia! You'll give everyone the impression that I'm an alcoholic the way you go on. I know I like the occasional brandy - but only after dinner.

Amelia   Yes, my darling, but you have twelve dinners each day.

Malcolm   *(with umbrage)* I'll have you know I'm very nearly teetotal!

Amelia   And *I'm* Angelina Jolie.

Malcolm   *(under his breath)* No such luck.

Amelia   What did you say?

Malcolm   Er... I said "Let's get on with the book".

Amelia   You know, you're too sensitive, Malcolm. I'm only pulling your leg about the brandy. It's only a little joke. You know that.. and Freddy knows that...

Malcolm   But there may be people listening who don't.

Amelia   Huh! Out here!? Miles from civilisation? Who could possibly hear us?

Malcolm   *(in a sinister voice)* You never know... Walls have ears, you know. *(Peers out at the audience)* And then there's the moors. Anyone could be out there... or even a whole group of people... *(More sinister)* Just sitting there..., staring at us from the dark... Just waiting... waiting for something to happen.

   (All three look intently towards the audience.)

Freddy   *(breaks the silence with a nervous cough)* Hmmm, well I'm sure it's only your imagination, Malcolm. And anyway, if anyone *is* watching us they'll soon get fed up just seeing the three of us talking.

Malcolm   Unless something... *(Dramatically) happens.*

Amelia   *(looks round nervously)* Like what, for instance?

Malcolm   *(sinister)* Like a *murder*, for instance...

   (There is a loud clap of thunder off. Freddy jumps nervously.)

Amelia   *(knowingly)* Oh, *I* see... It's going to be one of *those* plays, is it? Claps of thunder every time something sinister happens.

Malcolm   Got to let the "sound effects" chappies have their bit of fun, old girl.

Amelia   Yes, I suppose so.

Malcolm   *(to Freddy)* Anyway... come on, Freddy... back to the foul deed.

Freddy   *(looks round uneasily)* Must we? I've got a very bad feeling about all this.

Amelia   Don't let Malcolm worry you, Freddy. He's often like this. It all stems from having an infertile brain... Or did I mean *infantile?*

Malcolm   Just ignore her, Freddy. All women go through this sort of thing at Amelia's age, you know. They call it "The Change of Wife".

Amelia   He means "Change of Life".

Malcolm I *know* what I mean. Carry on, old man.

Freddy Well… all right, but any more of that thunder and I'm off. Go on, Malcolm. You were enthralling me with your day.

Malcolm That's right, so I was. Now, let's see… where was I?

Amelia In the bathroom. Repairing the damage from last night's excesses.

Malcolm Right. Next… down for breakfast. Same thing every morning, regular as clockwork. Two bowls of prunes, a bowl of muesli and a bowl of "All Bran"…,

Amelia As he said… regular as clockwork.

Malcolm …A glass of orange juice, a pair of kippers, a couple of eggs, bacon, fried bread, sausages, tomatoes and mushrooms, then rounding off with a few slices of toast and marmalade… if I'm still a peckish, that is.

Freddy Better cross "malnutrition" off my list of possible weapons, then.

Amelia How about adding a few pounds of senna pods to his prunes? He could die of…

Malcolm All right, Amelia! That'll do. This is a family show. We *don't* wish to know about that, thank you.

Amelia *(sulky)* Spoilsport.

Freddy I think we have to rule out poisons. They're too easily traced. *(Pensive)* No, it has to be something more subtle. Carry on with your day.

Malcolm OK. Let's see… after breakfast I always take a walk down by the river.

Freddy *(considers)* By the river, eh? Now that's got possibilities. You could easily slip in on a wet day and drown…, or the bank could collapse.

Malcolm The police would take some convincing about that one, old man. Remember I used to be the school swimming champion.

Freddy Yes, but if you were to hit your head on the way in, or something, so you were unconscious…

Amelia No good, I'm afraid, Freddy. Alcohol floats on water, you *know*.

Malcolm Amelia!

Freddy Well, what if I hit him when he's sober?

Amelia When he's *sober?* He hasn't been sober since he was seventeen!

Malcolm Amelia! Will you *please* stop going on about me being drunk...? Otherwise there'll be a *real* murder, and *you'll* be the victim! Now, can we please get back to the plot?

Freddy   Does anyone go with you on your walk?

Malcolm   Only Fifi and Mimi.

Freddy   Who?

Malcolm   Fifi and Mimi... The dogs.

Freddy   Is that what you call them... Fifi and Mimi!?

Malcolm   Yes. What's wrong with Fifi and Mimi?

Freddy   Well, two miniature poodles called Fifi and Mimi I could accept... But two enormous Irish Wolfhounds...!? I hate those dogs. They're evil. Every time they look at you, you can see it written in their eyes.

Amelia   See what?

Freddy   "Lunch".

Malcolm   Go on with you. They're soft as putty.

Freddy   No, I'm sorry Malcolm, I couldn't murder you when those two were around.

Amelia   But Freddy, don't you see? They'd be the perfect alibi!

Freddy   How d'you mean?

Amelia   Who would suspect anyone would be brave enough... or foolish enough... to bump off Malcolm when the dogs were there..? If you *could* find a way...

Freddy   Now look, you want it to be realistic, don't you? The dogs would be a dead giveaway. All the police would need to do would be to arrest the first man they came across who'd had both his arms ripped off at the shoulder.

Malcolm   Ah, yes, I take your point.

Freddy   Scratch the morning constitutional. What d'you do next?

Malcolm   Er... Back home for lunch. Mabel cooks an excellent salad.

Freddy   She *cooks* it!?

Amelia   Only the ham, Freddy. I know dear old Mabel is a little... how shall I put it...? Eccentric.., but even she draws the line at boiled lettuce.

Freddy   I'll never know why you don't get a proper cook. Letting a maid do all the food. She's so scatty... You could get poisoned and never know it till you woke up dead the next morning.

Amelia   You know, Freddy, you may have hit on an idea, there. Mabel poisons Malcolm without realising it. She could use poisonous mushrooms, or something, by accident.

Freddy   I'm sure it's been done before. Anyway, if I'm supposed to be having an affaire with you, how could I know that *you* wouldn't eat them too?

Amelia I could be in on it.

Freddy No, it would be too contrived.

Amelia Yes, you're right. Poison mushrooms have been done too many times before. What we need is something original, something that nobody would ever suspect. Make it look perfectly natural, or like an accident.

Freddy Yes... Or we could make sure all the possible suspects have perfect alibis. Perhaps they could all be together at the time, providing each other's alibis... Or in a public place.

Malcolm Well, we'll have to come up with something soon or the audience will start to nod off.

Freddy Yes, let's get a move on. Continue with your day, Malcolm.

Malcolm Well, now, let's think. Mondays, Wednesdays and Fridays I go to the Golf Club. The rest of the week I take it easy. These are the problems of being a kept man.

Freddy I'd change places with you any day. You sit around living the life of the landed gentry while poor old Amelia works herself to death writing her novels to support you.

Malcolm Steady on, old boy. I *do* help with the plots, you know.

Amelia Plots! That's an idea! Plots... We could bury you in your rose-beds.

Malcolm No good at all, I'm afraid, Amelia. My old faithfuls Fifi and Mimi would soon dig me up.

Amelia Those dogs are only faithful to the hand that feeds them, which in this case is Mabel. They'd probably help bury you, like they do with their other old bones.

Freddy Back to the Golf Course. What if you were to get hit on the head by a golf ball?

Amelia It would have to be a remarkably good shot.

Freddy (pensive) Yes, that's true. (Enthusiastic) Perhaps I could fire it from a catapult... or even from that old blunderbuss you keep hanging over the stairs.

Malcolm Now steady, Freddy. Whereas I would normally be the last one to pour cold water on a chap's ideas, you have to realise that this is a play we're doing, and on a pretty miserable budget, too. Those film wallahs can do wonders with their special effects, but we can't afford to have scenes set on golf courses or using fancy props like catapults and blunderbusses. You'll have to think of something a bit more ordinary.

Freddy Sorry, Malcolm. I got a bit carried away there.

Malcolm That's alright, old man. Just keep a grip on reality, that's all.

Amelia I reckon the best thing would be to bribe Smalls to do it.

Malcolm What!? The butler did it!? I'm surprised at you, Amelia. How corny can you get?

Amelia But don't you see? That's the beauty of it, no-one would suspect anything so obvious.

Malcolm *(derisory)* Smalls? *Smalls!?* What a load of...

Amelia *(stops him before he can say "Balls")* Malcolm!

Smalls *(enters L, carrying a glass. To Malcolm)* Did someone call, Sir?

Amelia No, Smalls, it was just Sir Malcolm taking your name in vain.

Smalls *(gives the brandy to Malcolm, takes the empty glass and turns away disdainfully.)* Very good, Ma'am.

Amelia Smalls, while you're here, would you do something for Mr Lyons and myself, please?

Smalls *(turns back towards Amelia)* Certainly, Madam. How may I be of service?

Amelia We'd like you to murder Sir Malcolm.

Smalls *(taken aback)* I... I beg your pardon, Madam. I er...

Malcolm Don't mind Her Ladyship, Smalls. She's trying to devise a plot for her new novel. It's called "How To Murder Your Husband In Front Of A Live Audience and Make It Entertaining".

Smalls From what I've heard so far, Sir, she's failed already.

Amelia Careful, Smalls... remember your position.

Smalls Sorry, Ma'am. Even though I'm the star of this play I had no desire to offend.

Amelia Apology accepted.

Malcolm You implied you could do better.

Smalls *(superior)* Better, Sir? Me, Sir? With what, may I enquire?

Malcolm With a murder plot. Come on, Smalls, out with it.

Smalls Begging your pardon, Sir. one would not presume...

Malcolm Of course you would. You butler chappies have a way of presuming without our ever realising it. Come on, Smalls, presume away. Let's hear how you'd devise the perfect crime.

Smalls Well, Sir. First of all, one must have the perfect alibi.

Amelia The perfect alibi? What d'you mean?

Smalls *(indicates the audience)* Out there, Ma'am. Dozens of faces, all watching.

Malcolm	*(dismissive)* Out there? We… er… we hadn't noticed.
Smalls	If one were able to perform the dastardly deed while *they* were all watching… but without them noticing, one could hardly be accused, could one?
Amelia	No, I suppose not. But how could you possibly murder someone with everybody watching?
Smalls	Well, firstly, I'd use a gun. That pistol you keep in the hall cabinet *(Indicates off R.)* would be ideal. Then I'd…
Mabel	*(off L)* Mr Smalls! Mr Smalls! Where are you?
Smalls	*(annoyed)* Oh no, what does she want now?
Mabel	*(enters L, wearing a cook's apron. Calls, brusque)* Mr Smalls! Mr *Smalls*! Oh, there you are.
Smalls	*(annoyed)* What is it, Mabel?
Mabel	How many times have I asked you to carry them tables down to the kitchen for me? How many times?
Smalls	I've no idea. I never was any good at times tables.
Mabel	I need them. And you promised.
Smalls	Not now, please, Mabel. I was just telling Lady Amelia how to murder Sir Malcolm.
Mabel	*(in one continuous sentence)* Well, I can't help that, I've got to have them tables in the.. what did you say?
Smalls	We're devising a plan to kill Sir Malcolm.
Mabel	*(to Smalls; trying not to let Malcolm hear)* Well, that's nice, isn't it..? It's bad enough that you're planning to do away with him, but to just come right out and say it in front of him like that… Not very polite, is it?
Malcolm	*(teasing)* Oh, it's all right, Mabel. I don't mind, really. I've had a good life, I can't complain. If that's how they feel, then so be it.
Mabel	*(moves to Malcolm and leans to him; concerned)* But Sir… how can you say that? You're still young. You can't just let them…
Amelia	Mabel, they're pulling your leg.
Mabel	*(confused)* They're what?
Freddy	We've been trying to devise a plot for Amelia's next novel, Mabel. Malcolm was only teasing you.
Mabel	*(straightens up; stares at Malcolm; indignant)* Oh, was he now? Well, Sir, I don't think that was very funny, do you?
Malcolm	Oh, come on, Mabel… surely you can take a joke? Where's your sense of humour?
Smalls	*(dryly)* What sense of humour?

Mabel	*(hands on hips; angry)* So! I've no sense of humour, now?
Amelia	*(to Malcolm)* Now you've done it.
Malcolm	Me!? I was only having a bit of fun. *(To Mabel)* Mabel, you know that, don't you?
Mabel	Hmmph! *(Turns to go; haughtily)* I'm going back to my kitchen. Dinner will be served… on Tuesday! *(Starts towards the door L; brusque)* Mr Smalls! *(Exits.)*
Smalls	*(follows her meekly)* Yes, Mabel.
Malcolm	*(looks after them)* Well, Freddy, old chap… it's back to you I'm afraid. The butler's busy, so he can't have done it.
Freddy	Where d'you go after golf?
Amelia	Nineteenth hole, of course. Malcolm always manages to get down in one at the nineteenth. *(Indicates drinking)* Several times a day.
Malcolm	You know, Amelia, instead of you and Freddy of bumping *me* off, maybe *I* should do away with *you*. There isn't a judge in the land'd commit me, y'know. Justifiable homicide if ever there was. I could get the pistol from the hall cabinet and…
Freddy	Why does everyone keep mentioning that pistol?
Amelia	You don't frighten me, Malcolm, darling. Most of the day you couldn't focus well enough to hit anything.
Freddy	Now steady on, you two. I don't want to be a part of your marital differences…
Amelia	Don't be a clot, Freddy. We're only joking. We wouldn't really harm a hair on each other's head. Would we, Malcolm?
Malcolm	Well, er… no… of course not.
Amelia	Although if Malcolm loses much more on top it'll be difficult to find any hair to harm. *(Malcolm instinctively puts his hand to the top of his head.)*
Malcolm	Just 'cause a chap's receding a bit… *(Takes a comb from pocket, dips it in his brandy and combs his hair.)*
Amelia	*(disgusted)* Malcolm!
Malcolm	What's that, old girl?
Amelia	No wonder you're going bald!
Malcolm	Button it up, old girl. You keep on using your mouth like that and you'll wear it out… *(Pleads to heaven)* please. Now, Freddy, what were we saying Freddy?
Freddy	You were going to say what you do after the golf.
Malcolm	Ah, yes. Back here for dinner.
Freddy	*(sarcastic)* Hard life you lead.

Malcolm	Yes, I know. Pressure, old man. Continuous pressure.

Malcolm   Yes, I know. Pressure, old man. Continuous pressure.

Freddy   What d'you have for your dinner?

Malcolm   Well, it varies, really...

(The doorbell rings off R.)

Amelia   I'll get it. *(Rises, she shouts to the door L)* Don't worry, Smalls, I'll go. You do the tables. *(Exits R.)*

Malcolm   *(looks at his watch)* I wonder who that can be.

Freddy   Probably the mad axe murderer.

Malcolm   No, he called last week. *(With a glance at his watch)* It's rather late for callers.

(Amelia, carrying a business card, returns followed by VIC, who is dressed in a raincoat.)

Amelia   Someone to see you, Malcolm. *(Reads card)* A Mister Tim.

Malcolm   *(reads card.)* Tim? That's an odd sort of name. *(Stands and shakes hands with Vic.)* Come in, old chap. Tim, eh...? That your first name or your last?

Vic   My last... My first's Vic.

Malcolm   Should I know you, Mr Tim?

Vic   Please, call me Vic. No, I don't think we've ever met.

Malcolm   *(pensive)* Vic Tim, eh? Very unusual name that. You involved in this play in some way, Vic?

Vic   Yes, I think so. I'm not exactly sure what I have to do. They've only given me a few lines, then I have to come back later as a policeman. It's all very confusing really.

Amelia   *(pensive)* Hmmm... Vic Tim, eh...? Vic Tim? You know, Vic, I think I may have an inkling of your role in tonight's little er... production. How many lines have you got, exactly?

Vic   Well... There's the one I'm speaking now, then two more.

Malcolm   Hmmm. Not much of a part, is it? Well, go on then, old chap... Make the most of it. The stage is yours.

Vic   Thanks. *(Moves R)* Well, first I have to go to this door over here, open it, and go out. *(Exits R.)*

Amelia   *(after he has gone)* Funny sort of chap.

(Smalls enters L.)

Malcolm   Yes, he was a bit odd. I wonder where he went?

Smalls   Perhaps he's just a red herring.

Freddy   Yes, he could be... put in by the scriptwriter to confuse everyone.

Amelia   Fairly successfully I'd say. I'm totally baffled.

Freddy   Yes, me too. I thought *I* was supposed to be bumping *you* off,

Malcolm.

Malcolm   Plenty of time, yet, old chap. There's still a couple of acts left. Don't go and ruin the plot.

Vic   *(off R)* ...Then I open the door again and come in... *(Enters R; moves C.)* ...and I move to the centre of the stage... *(Does so.)*

(A black-sleeved and gloved hand slowly appears through the open door R holding a large pistol. There is a very long burst of repeated shots aimed at Vic, who wriggles around dramatically as if being shot, eventually slides to the floor above C. With each shot they all flinch. The hand withdraws.)

Smalls   *(goes over to the prostrate body and peers at it; in his superior "butler" voice)* It's Mr Tim, Sir. I believe he may have been shot.

Malcolm   *(stands)* Shot!? Can you be sure?

Smalls   I'm fairly certain, Sir. There's a large pool of fake blood congealing on the carpet, and I believe I heard a recording of some gunfire a few moments ago. *(Stands upright.)*

Malcolm   Is he... *(Dramatically)* dead?

Smalls   *(leans over the body)* I'm no doctor, Sir, but a quick count shows thirty-two bullet wounds to the head and chest and a flesh wound to his left thumb. The odds are not in his favour. Though if I may say so, Sir, I thought it was very well acted.

Amelia   Yes, well acted, *John. (Alter to suit name of actor.)*

Malcolm   Hear! Hear! Good show, old man.

Freddy   Nice one, *John.*

(Amelia, Malcolm and Freddy applaud.)

Malcolm   *(to the audience)* Come on, you lot. Show a bit of appreciation.

(Vic stands and takes a bow to the audience. The hand appears at the door again and fires a single shot. Vic falls down again above C.)

Freddy   *(bright)* That's livened the whole thing up a bit, hasn't it?

Amelia   I'll say. I think the audience was expecting us to see you off, Malcolm, but now we've got a body there hardly seems any point.

Malcolm   Jolly good, too. It's about time I got a decent part.

Amelia   On the other hand, you'd better not relax too much, my darling. There *might* be two murders.

Freddy   Or more... *(Becomes pensive.)*

Malcolm   Yes, maybe you're right. Perhaps we'd better get this one

	solved so I can rest easy. *(To Smalls)* You know... *knew* him, did you, Smalls?
Smalls	Mr Tim... No, not really, Sir. Only from rehearsals. Who shot him, anyway?
Amelia	We don't know yet... And even if we did we're hardly going to tell you *now*, are we? We've still got two acts to go. If we wrap it up too soon we'll never sell any teas in the interval and the tea ladies'll be furious.
Malcolm	That's true. Smalls, you'd better ring for the police.
Smalls	*(turns to go)* Yes, Sir.
Amelia	*(pensive)* Smalls...
Smalls	Ma'am?
Amelia	Tell them not to send anyone *too* clever. We need about *(Looks at her watch)* another hour or so.
Malcolm	That incompetent French chappie'd be about right... Trousseau, or whatever he's called. The one in the "Pink Thingy".
Amelia	Clouseau.
Malcolm	That's the one.
Amelia	If we can't afford golf courses and catapults, we certainly can't afford him.
Malcolm	No, that's true. *(To Smalls)* Oh, just ask for a superior-sounding Inspector and a bumbling Detective Constable.
Smalls	Yes, Ma'am.
Malcolm	And while you're on, Smalls, tell them to send a pretty WPC. This play could do with a bit of glamour.
Smalls	Very good, Sir.
Amelia	*(after a pause; noticing a distracted Freddy)* You're very quiet, Freddy. Nothing wrong, is there?
Freddy	*(comes round)* Wrong? No, why should there be?
Amelia	I don't know. It's just that you've not said a word for ages.
Freddy	No, no, there's nothing wrong. That's just the way the script was written.
Malcolm	What about old Vic there? What shall we do?
Amelia	Yes. He makes the stage look awfully untidy just lying there.
Malcolm	Well, it's not the end of the scene for ages yet, so I suppose he'll just have to lie there.
Amelia	I hope he doesn't bleed all over my carpet. Mabel'll be furious.

Malcolm   *(steps over Vic and calls to off L)* Smalls!

Smalls   *(enters R)* Sir?

Malcolm   Go and fetch a plastic sheet or something, will you? Slide it under *(With distaste) that.*

Smalls   Yes, Sir. *(Exits L.)*

        (Malcolm steps back over Vic.)

Amelia   No, wait a minute. We can't have him lying there all the act getting in the way. And anyway, he's playing another part later on, so he'll have to go off and get changed.

Freddy   But he can't just get up and walk off. He's supposed to be dead. The audience will suspect.

Malcolm   *(looks towards the audience)* Yes, I'd forgotten about them. Dashed nuisance. Mind you, looking at this lot they'll probably never notice. *(Surveys the audience)* Look at them… a sea of blank stares. It looks like Southport beach when the tide's out.

Amelia   Look, I know this lot are not exactly intellectual giants… After all, they came here tonight…, but I don't imagine they think he's *really* dead.

        (Vic holds up a small sign saying "Hello Mum".)

Malcolm   That's beside the point. He *can't* just walk off.

Amelia   How about if we wait till they drop off to sleep?

Malcolm   Yes, that's an idea.

        (Amelia and Freddy sit and nervously look around for a short while, twiddling thumbs, etc., while Malcolm wanders nonchalantly round the room, stepping over Vic now and again. They occasionally glance at the audience.)

Malcolm   *(eventually)* It's not working, Amelia. We'll have to think of something else.

Freddy   I know… I'll create a diversion.

Amelia   Who d'you think you are, a road mender?

Freddy   No, I mean I'll… I'll sing them a song.

Amelia   No! Don't do that for goodness sake. *(Points at exit doors.)* Those doors aren't locked… they'd all leave.

Malcolm   What if we stand in front of him and hide him from the audience? He could sort of… sidle off behind us. *(Stands and moves towards Vic.)* Come on…, both of you.

        (Amelia and Freddy stand and try - unsuccessfully - to hide Vic from the audience.)

Amelia   It's no good, Malcolm. We need something bigger. We'll have to think of something else.

Freddy	What if we use the sofa?
Malcolm	Hmmm. Might be worth a try. Come on, Freddy, give me a hand.

(Malcolm and Freddy take one end of the sofa each and carry it in front of Vic, where they put it down.)

Vic	*(from behind the sofa; as they put it down)* Ow!
Malcolm	*(to Vic, behind the sofa)* Sorry, old chap. You ready…? *(To Freddy)* After three, then. *(Takes a position at the end of the sofa again, smiling at the audience. In a tight-lipped voice)* One… two… *three.*

(Malcolm and Freddy lift the sofa and move slowly L, look and smile at the audience. VIC creeps stealthily out R. They replace the sofa where it was.)

Malcolm	There! That's much better.
Freddy	D'you think anyone noticed?
Malcolm	No, I don't think so. Even *I* didn't see him go.
Amelia	What shall we do now?
Malcolm	Wait for the police, I suppose.

(They all sit bored and nervous looking about them.)

Amelia	*(eventually)* Fancy a cup of tea?
Malcolm	Yes, that'd be nice.
Amelia	Freddy?
Freddy	Rather.
Amelia	*(rises)* Come on, then.

(Amelia, Freddy and Malcolm exit L. A few moments later Smalls enters R, and, seeing no-one in the room, crosses to L and calls through the door.)

Smalls	Mabel…! Mabel, are you there?
Mabel	*(off L)* What is it now, Mr Smalls?

(Mabel enters L. Her right hand is firmly stuck to a plateful of pastry. At various points until she next exits she attempts unsuccessfully to pull the plate from her hand.)

Mabel	I've got pastry to do. I think I must have used too many eggs.
Smalls	*(ushers her in)* Mabel, come in. Sit down a minute. I want to talk to you.
Mabel	*(sits, then starts to rise again defensively)* If it's about that bottle of sherry, it wasn't me… honest. I wasn't there when I did it!
Smalls	*(puzzled)* What!?
Mabel	*(sits back again)* It was Rover.

Smalls	Rover...?
Mabel	He adores sherry, that cat.
Smalls	*(impatient)* Mabel, what are you talking about?
Mabel	You said you wanted to talk to me about the missing sherry.
Smalls	No I didn't.
Mabel	Well, anyway... it wasn't me.
Smalls	*(tired of this)* Now look, Mabel. I am not in the least bit interested if you happen borrow a nip or two of Lady Amelia's sherry every now and again.
Mabel	You're not?
Smalls	You can bath in the stuff as far as I'm concerned.
Mabel	Oooh, what a lovely idea.
Smalls	I wanted to talk to you about the Master and Lady Amelia.
Mabel	What about them?
Smalls	Well, they've been behaving very strangely lately. You must have noticed.
Mabel	Strangely...? How d'you mean?
Smalls	Well, for example... Only the other day I went in the study and Lady Amelia was at the Master's desk.
Mabel	So? I don't see...
Smalls	She didn't hear me enter at first. I did my polite butler's cough *(Cups his hand to his mouth; by way of example)* Ahem! ...and she jumped up like a scared rabbit.
Mabel	I'm not at all surprised, the way you're always creeping round the place. That's why I put them drawing pins in the soles of your shoes that time... So they'd make a noise an I could hear you before you caught me at Lady Amelia's sherry. Not that I do, of course.
Smalls	*(losing his cool)* Will you shut up about the sherry, woman? This is serious.
Mabel	Sorry, Mr Smalls. Carry on.
Smalls	Lady Amelia was looking at some papers. She tried to hide them when she saw me, but I noticed what they were.
Mabel	And...?
Smalls	*(looks from side to side to check nobody is within earshot; dramatically)* Insurance policies. *(Mabel, without knowing why, also looks from side to side as Smalls did.)*
Mabel	Go on with your...
Smalls	*(checks again) Life* insurance policies.

Mabel	Well I never...
Smalls	And *all* taken out on Sir Malcolm.
Mabel	All? How many were there?
Smalls	Well, quite a few.
Mabel	How did you know they were all for His Lordship?
Smalls	I er... happened to notice one day when I was... er...
Mabel	Snooping around.
Smalls	No... I, er... I was checking the windows were locked.
Mabel	Even so... what does that prove? Lots of people have life insurance policies.
Smalls	All dated last week?
Mabel	What are you suggesting?
Smalls	I think she wants to do away with him.
Mabel	Oooh, Mr Smalls, how can you? Don't even suggest such a thing.
Smalls	Mark my words, Mabel. Something fishy's going on in this house. Something sinister and evil. I think there's going to be a murder before the night's out.
Mabel	*(with a shudder)* Oooh, Mr Smalls... that's horrible... Here, I hope nobody murders me. *(Pensive)* I'm sure I wouldn't like it. I'd much rather it was somebody else... You, for example.
Smalls	*(sarcastic)* Your devotion touches me, Mabel. I never knew you cared.
Mabel	You know what I mean, Mr Smalls. I just don't want to be murdered, that's all. I bet it hurts a lot..., and anyway, I don't want to die yet... I've still got three weeks to go on my Open University course.
Smalls	*(after a defeated shake of the head)* It's a pity you didn't take a course in Private Detection... or Forensic Science. If my suspicions are correct, those might become useful.
Mabel	*(dismissive)* I'm sure it's just your imagination, Mr Smalls. You know Lady Amelia and Sir Malcolm are always going on about murder plots for her books... It's probably just another one of those.
Smalls	*(dubious)* Maybe so, but I still think...
Mabel	Mind you, just yesterday Sir Malcolm was in the kitchen checking his supplies of cooking brandy, and he made some remark about weedkiller... But I'm sure he was only joking...
Smalls	Yes, probably. He always calls your soups "weedkiller".
Mabel	*(looks hurt)* Why does he?
Smalls	Apparently he once spilt some on his Venus' Flytrap...

Mabel   *(shocked)* On his *what*!?

Smalls   You know… that disgusting plant in the dining room that eats flies when they land on it.

Mabel   And?

Smalls   It spat it out.

Mabel   I don't believe you.

Smalls   That's what the master said.

Mabel   I don't take no notice of what he says. He's always kidding me is Sir Malcolm. I never know how to take him. He could tell me snow's red and I'd have to go outside and check before I was sure.

Smalls   You were happy enough to believe he was joking about the weedkiller, though.

Mabel   *(shivers; nervous)* Now stop it, Mr Smalls. You've got me all jumpy. The way you're talking you'd think everybody's trying to murder everybody else.

Smalls   It's possible.

Mabel   What possible motive could Sir Malcolm have to murder Her Ladyship?

Smalls   Perhaps *he's* got insurance on *her*. She's a wealthy woman, you know… Then again, perhaps he thinks like we do.

Mabel   What d'you mean?

Smalls   Maybe he thinks *she's* planning to do away with *him*, so he's trying to get in first.

Mabel   *(shivers)* Oooh! It doesn't bear thinking about… What are we going to do? If Lady Amelia *is* planning to murder the master, we can't just stand by and let it happen, can we?

Smalls   No, I agree. But what can we do? We can hardly just come right out and say "Your afternoon tea, Ma'am. Oh, and by the way, shall I set one less place for dinner?"!

Mabel   No, that's true. Perhaps we could sort of *hint* at it… drop a few suggestions and see how they react.

Smalls   It might be worth a try…

Mabel   Look out! There's someone coming.
              (They both exit hurriedly R.)

Amelia   *(enters L. Looks in surprise at the audience.)* Still here? Your tea'll be getting cold. You go through that little door there and get your tea, there's good people. *(Exits L. As she exits; to off L)* Close that blasted curtain, for goodness' sake.
                              The curtain falls

ACT II

(As the curtain rises, the stage is empty. Inspector Sides enters L. She is smartly dressed in a dark suit. She stops just inside the door and surveys the room grimly.)

Sides *(calls to off L)* Come along, Detective Constable! In here.

Fickey *(off L)* Coming, Inspector!

(DC Fickey enters breathlessly L. He wears a similar coloured suit and is trying to put his shoes on as he enters. He looks nervously at where he had been lying. After a moment he looks curiously at Sides.)

Sides Ah, there you are, D.C. Fickey.

Fickey *(snaps to attention)* Sir!

Sides Now, Constable, what I want you to do is...

Fickey *(looks at her curiously)* Excuse me, Inspector... Are you alright?

Sides Of course, Fickey, why shouldn't I be?

Fickey Well, er... it's just... *(Pause.)* Could you come over here a second? *(Tries to turn her upstage.)*

Sides *(resists)* What the devil are you doing?

Fickey Please, Inspector. Just humour me.

Sides Oh, very well.

(Sides allows herself to be turned upstage, her back to the audience. Fickey goes round to the front of her and opens her jacket. His look of curiosity turns to one of amazement.)

Sides Anything wrong, Detective Constable?

Fickey *(Still looking)* No... Everything looks perfect to me. Except that... well... if you don't mind me saying so, Sir, you're not a sir, Sir... You're a *Mrs Sir*, sir.

Sides Very observant, Fickey... and the term is "Ma'am".

Fickey Yes, Sir... Ma'am. Sorry, Ma'am. *(Confused)* I'm sure you were a sir in the script.

Sides Well, as you can see I'm not. Now perhaps we can get on with the investigation. *(Closes her jacket and turns downstage.)*

Fickey You been in the Force long, Ma'am?

Sides No, I was drafted in last night. They wanted a man, but I failed the physical. Now, can we *please* get on with it?

Fickey Anything you say... Ma'am.

Sides Good. *(Looks round the room)* This room, Fickey, is where the dreadful deed was perpetrated.

Fickey   Yes, Inspector Ma'am, Sir. I know.

Sides   *(surprised)* You *know*...? How do *you* know?

Fickey   Well, Ma'am, perhaps I don't exactly *know* as such. It's just a feeling I keep having... a sort of vision. Like an experience from a previous life.

Sides   Déjà vu?

Fickey   No thank you Ma'am. I don't like foreign food.

Sides   I sometimes wonder how you ever got into the Police Force, DC Fickey. It's even more amazing how you ever got a promotion.

Fickey   *(with pride)* That's easy, Ma'am. I'm related to the Producer.

Sides   Yes... well never mind that now. We've got a murder to solve. Where's WPC Nunnall?

Fickey   Following on later, Ma'am. She had to do some shopping.

Sides   *(furious) What!?* Shopping!? *Shopping!!?* What *is* this Police Force coming to? Shopping during office hours!? Wait till I see her, I'll...

Fickey   *(interrupts)* Something about an anniversary present, Ma'am.

Sides   A *what!!?*

Fickey   For your wife, Ma'am. Or was it your husband?

Sides   What? Ah! Oh... Oh, yes. I forgot... Well, if it's official Police business I'll overlook it. Just this once, mind.

Fickey   Very noble of you, I'm sure, Ma'am.

Sides   Now..., to business, constable.

Fickey   Ma'am?

Sides   Start looking around.

Fickey   Yes, Ma'am...

(Sides and Fickey start to look round the room. Fickey looks in the most unlikely places, such as the soles of his shoes, inside glasses, on light switches, etc.)

Fickey   *(stops and looks up)* Inspector, Ma'am...

Sides   *(continues)* What is it, Constable?

Fickey   What exactly are we looking for?

Sides   *(looks up in amazement)* For clues, of course.

(Both resume their search.)

Fickey   Ah... clues... right. *(Looks around some more and finds Malcolm's newspaper in the armchair. It is open at the crossword. Picks it up and looks at it.)* Here's a clue, Ma'am.

Sides   *(moves down R; still searching)* Well done, Fickey. What is it?

Fickey	It says, "Sweet made from fruit and custard. Four letters."
Sides	What are you talking about…? *(Sees the newspaper; angry)* Fool!
Fickey	*(puzzled)* Fool? *(Eventually)* Oh, yes…, fool. That's right! You are clever, Ma'am. Got a pen?
Sides	Fickey! Put that paper down and look for clues… to the murder!
Fickey	*(reluctantly puts the paper down; sulky)* Yes, Ma'am. *(They continue. Sides arrives below C and looks out over the moors. She is impressed by the scene and stops to admire it.)*
Sides	*(dreamy)* Ah… Isn't it peaceful out here, Constable Fickey? So much nicer than the city. Just think about it… a life of leisure…, no pressure…, no rushing around…, no wailing sirens…, and just look at that view over the moors. Imagine waking up to that view every day. I'd love to retire somewhere like this.
Fickey	*(still searching in the most unlikely places)* Not me, Ma'am. Drive me crackers out here. Give me the city any day of the week. A nice friendly little pub on the corner…, a few beers with the lads on a Friday…, nightclubs, bars, dances…, a little punch-up every now and again…, *(moves towards Sides; getting enthusiastic)* some collars to feel…, some heads to bang…, some legs to break…
Sides	Now, now, Detective Constable Fickey, control yourself. You don't want to bring on your headaches again. You know what happened last time. No more violence, please.
Fickey	*(sulky)* What? Not even a little bit?
Sides	Not even a smidgen.
Fickey	You mean to say we've come out all this way and I don't get to *(Punches his hand)* interrogate nobody?
Sides	Definitely not. You have to realise we're dealing with the upper classes here. You can't go around *(with a similar punch)* interrogating them. You've got to be polite, gentle and diplomatic.
Fickey	Diplomatic? What's that mean?
Sides	It means… Oh, never mind. Just let *me* do the talking.
Fickey	But, Ma'am…
Sides	Can't you curb your animal tendencies for once, Fickey? *(Looks over the moors again)* Just come and have a look out there… Doesn't this place affect you at all… make you feel at

	peace with life…?
Fickey	*(puzzled)* Eh?
Sides	*(grandly)* Just stop for a few seconds and appreciate the moment. Cast your eyes out across the moors… breathe that air… *(Breathes in deeply.)*
Fickey	*(sniffs)* Smells like manure to me.
Sides	You just don't appreciate the good things in life, do you, Detective Constable? You ought to… *(Suddenly notices something on the moors. Tense)* Wait a minute… What was that?
Fickey	What was what?
Sides	*(points)* Out there… on that hillock…
Fickey	*(sotto voce)* Mind your language, Ma'am… children present.
Sides	I said *"hillock"*, Constable. I thought I saw someone.
Fickey	*(peers)* Someone? Out there?
Sides	*(dramatically)* Someone… or some*thing*.
	(Sides and Fickey look at each other nervously, then back at the moors.)
Sides	*(suddenly points again)* There! There it was again! Did you see it?
Fickey	*(nervously)* Yes Ma'am, I think I did see something. What d'you think it was?
Sides	I don't know… but I didn't like the look of it at all. It didn't look very… *human.*
Fickey	D'you think that's what did the murder, Ma'am?
Sides	You may be right, Fickey.
	(They exchange more nervous glances.)
Fickey	I don't think I like it here, Ma'am. Can we go now?
Sides	Certainly not! We've a murder to solve.
Fickey	But Ma'am… It's getting foggy, and it might rain, and I've not brought my mac… anyway, I'll have to be getting home… I left a quiche in the oven.
Sides	Courage, Fickey, courage.
Fickey	Quick, Ma'am. Move away from the window. It might see us. We should have come armed.
	(Both move back as if hiding behind the "curtains".)
Mabel	*(enters L. moves towards them; deadpan)* What are you two doing?
Sides	*(holds up an arm to bar her path; hushed)* Keep back, Ma'am! There's someone… some*thing*… out there on the moors.

Fickey	And it ain't human.
Mabel	*(pushes through them and goes to the "window")* Don't be ridiculous. Let me look.
Fickey	*(points suddenly)* There! It moved again. It looks *horrible*. Did you see it?
Mabel	*(matter-of-fact)* Yes, 'course I saw it. You never seen one o' them before?
Sides	Never! Only in nightmares! Have you?
Mabel	Course I 'ave. Loads'a times. You get them all the time here.
Sides	You do? Then what is it?
Mabel	*(speaks as if to simpletons)* It's an *audience*.
Sides	A what?
Mabel	An audience… People… Ladies and gentlemen.
	(Fickey and Sides suddenly and immediately return to absolute normality.)
Sides	*(relieved)* Oh, that's alright, then.
Fickey	*(macho)* O.K. Fine. An audience… of course.
Mabel	Who *are* you anyway?
Sides	Police, Ma'am. Inspector Sides.
Mabel	Insecticides?
Sides	Detective Inspector Dianne Sides of Dee-on-Sea Criminal Investigation Division at your service.
Mabel	Beg pardon?
Sides	Inspector Dianne Sides. Dee-on-Sea CID. *(Pulls a card from her pocket and hands it to Mabel.)* My I.D.
Mabel	*(reads)* "D.I. D.Sides, Dee-on-Sea CID". *(Hands back the card)* I see… *(to Fickey)* And who're you?
Fickey	*(moves to Mabel)* I'm Fickey.
Mabel	*(looks him up and down)* Yes… you look it.
Sides	And you must be Lady Amelia.
Mabel	No I mustn't. I'm Mabel… Housekeeper, cook and maid to Sir Malcolm and Lady Simpson-Squire.
Fickey	*(moves towards her; menacing)* Where were you on the night of the alleged murder?
Mabel	*(stands her ground)* *Alleged* murder!? *Alleged* murder!? What else could it have been? Would have to be a very determined suicide to shoot himself that many times.
Fickey	*(attacks)* How did you know it was a shooting? *I* never said it was a shooting.
Mabel	Alright, then… have it your way. It was a stabbing. With a

knife that went bang, bang, bang... bang, bang..., bang-bang-bang, bang...

Fickey *(still menacing)* Stop trying to change the subject. Answer the question.

Mabel Don't you speak to *me* like that. I'll fetch you one round the ear.

Fickey *(to Sides)* Is she allowed to do that, Ma'am?

Sides Shut up, Fickey. *(To Mabel)* Please, Miss, ignore him. Sit down. *(Mabel sits on the settee. To Fickey; sotto voce)* I told you, Fickey. Upper classes. Softly, softly. Now shut up.

Fickey Yes, Ma'am.

Sides *(turns to Mabel)* Good... Now perhaps...

Fickey Shutting up at once, Ma'am.

Sides *(turns back)* Fickey...!

(Fickey stops speaking and tries to look innocent. Sides glares at him suspiciously. They pause, Sides glaring and Fickey looking angelic.)

Fickey *(as Sides looks away and is about to speak to Mabel)* Immediately, Ma'am.

Sides *(furious)* FICKEY! *(Stamps on his toe.)*

Fickey *(hops up and down in pain)* Oh, Ma'am! Right on my corn!

Sides Sorry about that, Miss. DC Fickey here gets a little er... carried away sometimes.

Mabel Pity someone doesn't carry him away now.

Sides Carry on searching, Fickey.

(Fickey limps and continues searching round the room again, not listening to the lines that follow.)

Sides Now, Miss, perhaps if you could answer one or two little questions.

Mabel *(sits)* Doubt it. I don't know nothing about nothing.

Sides Were you in the room when the murder occurred?

Mabel No, I was in the little room.

Sides *(to Fickey)* Are you taking notes, DC Fickey?

Fickey *(distracted)* Beg pardon, Ma'am?

Sides *(impatient)* I said "Are you taking notes?"

Fickey *(suddenly looks up; defensive)* Taking notes, Ma'am? Me, Ma'am? No, Ma'am. Never taken a bribe in my life! Whoever said I did was a liar, Ma'am, and I'll break every bone...

Sides *(interrupts; exasperated)* I don't mean *five pound* notes, Fickey. I mean notes in your notebook.

Fickey   Oh, I see, Ma'am. Right away, Ma'am. *(Takes a notebook from his pocket and starts searching his pockets for a pen.)*

Sides   Now, Miss… you were in the little room when Mr Tim met his untimely death. Describe to me, if you will, anything you saw.

Mabel   Nothing. I didn't see nothing.

Fickey   *(comes towards her, menacing again)* Nothing!? How can you be in the room when somebody's shot nineteen times and not see anything?

Mabel   I didn't! I wasn't!

Fickey   *(menacing)* I think she's lying, Ma'am. *(Advances on Mabel)* Want me to try an arm lock?

Mabel   *(stands)* Want me to try a swift kick in the groin?

Sides   I don't want to have to tell you again, Fickey. Silence! Notes!

Fickey   But…

Mabel   Silence!

(Fickey gives Mabel a menacing look, which she returns. Unseen by Sides, Fickey pulls a tongue. Mabel does likewise.)

Sides   Sorry about that, Miss. So, you didn't see anything?

Mabel   No. Nothing.

Fickey   She said she was in the room, Ma'am. She must have seen something.

Mabel   I wasn't in *this* room, you stupid man!

Fickey   *(threatening)* Now listen you! I may be stupid, but I'm *not* a man! Now, were you in the room or not?

Mabel   I was in the smallest room. You know - the privy. The *(whispers)* toilet.

Sides   Oh, yes, I see.

Fickey   *(suspicious)* The toilet!? A likely story. Anyone in there with you to substantiate your alibi, Miss?

Mabel   *(to Fickey)* Were you born stupid, or did you have to go to a special school?

Fickey   *(defensive)* I'll have you know, Miss, most people say I don't look nearly as stupid as I am. *(With a sneer)* So there!

Mabel   *(shakes head in defeat)* Oh, I give up.

Fickey   *(to Mabel, menacing)* Give up!? Give up, do you? *(Self-satisfied)* I knew you'd confess in the end. I knew it was you all along. *(To Sides)* I knew it was her, Ma'am. She's got shifty eyes, that one. Never trust anyone with shifty eyes.

Sides   DC Fickey…

Fickey	Ma'am?
Sides	Shut up, DC Fickey… Again.
Fickey	Yes, Ma'am… Again.
Sides	*(to Mabel)* Did you know the man who was shot?
Mabel	No, Mum.
Sides	Ever seen him before?
Mabel	No, Mum. Only *after.*
Sides	*(puzzled)* What…? After…?
Mabel	Yes, Mum. After he was killed. Came running back into the dressing room tearing his clothes off and rabbitting on about changing into a policeman.
	(Single gunshot off R. Mabel, Sides and Fickey stop talking and look up concerned.)
Sides	*(nervous)* What was that?
Fickey	*(nervous)* I think it may have been… a gunshot, Ma'am. *(There is a clap of thunder.)*
Sides	I *know* that, Fickey. I meant… Oh, never mind. *(Points off R)* Go and investigate.
Fickey	What? Me, Ma'am? Isn't this a job for the Police?
Sides	We *are* the Police.
Fickey	Oh yes, I forgot.
Sides	Off you go, then.
Fickey	*(not moving)* Er… On my own?
Sides	Yes. Don't tell me a big strong Detective Constable like you is afraid of a teeny-weeny gunshot.
Fickey	*(stands to attention; bravely)* Me, Ma'am? *(Pauses, uneasy)* Yes, Ma'am… terrified.
Sides	Detective Constable Fickey! I am your superior officer. That was an order. Now go!
Fickey	Isn't it a woman's job, Ma'am?
Sides	No! It's *your* job. You will do as you are told. Now *go!*
Fickey	*(hesitant)* I've got a very bad feeling about this, Ma'am.
Sides	*(stands and points to the door; firmly)* GO!
	(Fickey turns towards the door R.)
Mabel	*(taunting; sarcastic)* Bye, bye, Detective Constable. If I don't see you before you… er… depart… I'll be delighted.
Fickey	*(turns towards Mabel; to Sides)* Can't I just thump her a bit before I go, Ma'am? Get the adrenalin going?
Sides	*(points)* GO!!! *(Stamps on his foot again.)*
Fickey	*(hops)* Ow! Ma'am, d'you have to keep doing that?

Sides	Yes. It's in the script, and anyway I enjoy it.
	(Fickey limps nervously to the door R, opens it and gingerly peers out. He turns to talk to Sides, but seeing her stern face, thinks better of it and exits.)
Sides	Now, Mabel. Where were we...?
Mabel	You were asking if I knew Mr Tim, Mum, and I was telling you...
Sides	Oh, yes, that's right. Now, have you seen anyone acting suspiciously around here recently?
Mabel	Yes, Mum.
Sides	*(eager)* Really...? Who?
Mabel	Why, everyone, Mum.
Sides	Everyone?
Mabel	Yes, Mum... the whole cast's been acting suspiciously if you ask me.
Sides	How do you mean?
Mabel	P'raps I should put it another way, Mum. I've had a *suspicion* that the whole cast has been *acting*... But then again, I could be wrong.
Sides	No, Mabel. I *do* see what you mean, but that wasn't what I meant. I'm...
Fickey	*(rushes in R in a panic)* Inspector Sides, Ma'am... Inspector Sides.
Sides	*(annoyed at being interrupted)* What is it now, Fickey?
Fickey	There's been another murder, Ma'am.
	(Mabel and Sides both gasp. There is a clap of thunder off.)
Sides	What...? But who?
Fickey	The Producer, Ma'am.
Mabel	*What!?* Somebody's murdered the Producer?
Fickey	Yes. He's on the dressing room floor, Ma'am. It's... it's *horrible.*
Sides	Oh, it's not that bad. A new carpet and it'd look perfect. Any clue as to who did it?
Fickey	Yes, Ma'am. *He* did it.
Sides	*(impatient)* He...? Who's "he"?
Fickey	The Producer, Ma'am. He murdered *himself.* It was in the manner of a self-inflicted suicide.
Sides	*(pensive)* So *that's* what the gunshot was...
Fickey	That's right, Ma'am... He poisoned himself.
Sides	What...? How?

Fickey	Some sort of poison in his tea in the interval as far as I can make out, Ma'am.
Sides	What!!? But... but... that's ridiculous. *We* had that tea as well, and we're alright.
Mabel	*(aside; indicates Fickey) He's* not!
Fickey	No, Ma'am. We had *our* tea in the dressing room. The Producer had his out of the *main* pot.
Sides	*(horrified)* The *main* pot!? You mean...? *(Stops in horror.)*
Fickey	Yes, Ma'am. I'm afraid so.
Mabel	What? What is it?
Sides	The audience! They had theirs out of that pot. *(Fickey moves down stage and peers towards the audience.)* Oh, my goodness, what are we going to do? If anything should happen to them...
Fickey	I think we're too late, Ma'am.
Sides	What!?
Fickey	*(bows his head in reverence)* Look at them, Ma'am. They're all... *(Hand on heart; dramatically)* gone.
Mabel	Oh, no... not again. I *told* you we should have locked the doors...
Fickey	I don't mean gone, I mean *gone*!... They've... passed on.
Sides	*(panicky)* Oh, good grief! What can we do..? Are we insured for this sort of thing?
Fickey	No, Ma'am. We're only insured for fire... *(After a thought)* Perhaps if I were to nip down to the front row and... Have you a match on you, Ma'am? *(Points to the end of the front row in the audience)* Perhaps if I lit the one on the end there it would spread to the rest, and we could claim...
Mabel	No, you can't do that! It's "No Smoking" in here! You'll have to go and organise a skip, then we can... *(Suddenly; pointing at the audience)* Wait a minute! One of them yawned! We may be in time! Fetch an ambulance, quickly... *(Fickey and Sides start to move towards the L and R exits, but cannot get past each other. Suddenly points somewhere else in the audience)* No, wait. Another one moved. *(All three peer out at the audience, then relax slightly.)*
Sides	*(relieved)* Oh, thank goodness for that... they're only sleeping. I thought for a minute we'd killed them all.
Mabel	*(a little upset; sulky)* If they *had* got poisoned it would've served them right!
Sides	Why? What've they ever done to upset you?

Mabel   Well.., it's all *their* fault, isn't it?

Sides   What is?

Mabel   The poor old Producer.

Fickey   What!? *(Menacing)* Did *they* do it? Shall I go down and sort
them out, Ma'am? *(Moves below C and looks menacingly at
the audience.)*

Sides   *(still concerned with Mabel)* Be quiet, Fickey! *(To Mabel)* Why
is it *their* fault?

Mabel   Well..., he tried his best, didn't he? He worked very hard to
put this play on, you know..., spent long hours getting us all
in shape. The least *they* could've done is laughed every now
and again..., shown a little appreciation. It wouldn't have hurt
them. *(Accusingly, to the audience)* Beasts!

Sides   *(hand on Mabel's shoulder; calming)* Now, steady on, Mabel.
You can't blame them. It didn't say it was a comedy on the
posters, and nothing we've done so far tonight will have given
them any clues. It's not their fault..

Mabel   *(with a sigh)* Yes... I suppose you're right. *(To the audience;
emotional)* Look, I'm sorry, all of you... I didn't mean... It's
just that I was very fond of the Producer. We were very close.
He's always been... not just a colleague and a friend... *(sob)*
more like... like a distant cousin twice removed to me.
(Thoroughly miserable; with a sob) I don't think I'll ever get
over it... *(Gives another sob. Then, suddenly bright and
dismissive)* Then again, I suppose we could always get
somebody else to produce the next play.
(Amelia, Freddy and Malcolm enter L.)

Amelia   *(to Sides and Fickey)* And whom, may one ask, are you?

Sides   Inspector Sides at your service, Ma'am.

Malcolm   Insecticides?

Mabel   )

Sides   ) *(together)* We've already done that one!

Fickey   )

Mabel   *(urgently)* Someone's killed the Producer, Ma'am?

Amelia   What!? How?

Fickey   Some sort of poison, Ma'am. Fly killer of some kind, I'd
guess.

Amelia   Insecticides?

Sides   You called, Ma'am?

Malcolm   Now, we hadn't done *that* one!

Amelia   I assume these are the police, Malcolm.

Malcolm	Oh, I see. Which one's this French fellow… Inspector *Trousseau*, or whatever he's called?
Freddy	That's Inspector *Close-Up*, old man.
Fickey	*(takes a card out of his pocket with great flourish and giving it to Malcolm; with a superior look at Sides)* My card.
	(Malcolm looks Fickey up and down, and does obviously not like what he sees.)
Malcolm	*(reads with distaste)* DC V.Fickey, Dee-on-Sea CID. I see. What does the "V" stand for?
Fickey	*(proudly)* My first name.
Malcolm	I realised that! But what *is* your first name?
Fickey	Vic.
Malcolm	Vic, eh? That's one hell of a coincidence. Same as that other chappie - the one who was shot. As a matter of fact you look *remarkably* like him, old man. Is that why you're called Vic as well?
Sides	No, sir. He's called Vic because he gets right up everybody's nose. *(Very politely)* And may one presume to enquire…?
Amelia	Yes…?
Fickey	*(not politely)* Who're you?
Amelia	I'm Lady Amelia Simpson-Squire.
	(Offers her hand to Sides, who shakes it. Fickey extends his hand similarly. Amelia looks at his hand with distaste and ignores it.)
Amelia	My friends call me Amelia.
Fickey	My friend calls me Vicky.
Malcolm	*(curious)* Vicky Fickey!?
Amelia	*(to Fickey)* You may call me "Lady Simpson-Squire". *(To Sides)* This is my late husband, Sir Malcolm…
Malcolm	*(surprised)* What do you mean, "late"?
Amelia	*(puts her hand to her mouth)* Ooops, sorry, darling. Getting a little ahead of the plot, there.
Malcolm	*(uneasy)* Amelia… Do you know something I don't?
Amelia	*(strokes his cheek; teasing)* Wait and see, my darling, wait and see. *(To Sides; correcting herself)* This is my *husband*, Sir Malcolm Squire, Lord of the Manor, Master of the Hounds, Supporter of the bar and *gourmet par flatulence*.
Malcolm	Now look here, Amelia…
	(Doorbell rings off R. Smalls enters L and walks briskly across to exit R.)

Amelia	And this is Freddy Lyons, a friend. And that was Smalls, the Butler.
Fickey	*(to himself)* A butler, eh? I bet *he* did it.
	(Smalls re-enters R followed by WPC Eve Nunnall. She wears a very sexy version of a Police Uniform, with a rakishly-angled hat, black handbag, black stockings and high heels.)
Amelia	*(slightly disapproving)* And I've no idea who this is…
Malcolm	*(looks up slowly)* Who…? *(Suddenly notices Eve and starts to show a great deal of interest)* I say…!
Sides	Ah, here at last, Constable. This is Sir Malcolm and Lady Squire, and this is Mr Lyons, and over here we have Mabel. *(To everyone; indicates Eve)* This is WPC Nunnall.
Malcolm	*(sidles up to Eve; extending his hand)* Delighted to meet you, WPC Nunnall. *(Grandly kisses her hand, and does not let go)* Please call me Malc.
Amelia	*(in disbelief)* Malc…!?
Eve	Pleased to meet you, Sir Malcolm. Please… call me Eve.
Malcolm	That's a pretty name… Eve… Eve Nunnall…?
Sides Fickey	} *(together; with a "policeman's dip")* Evenin' all.
Amelia	*(exasperated)* You mean to say they've called you Eve Nunnall, just so…
Sides Fickey	} *(together; again)* Evenin' all.
Amelia	*(gives an exasperated look towards Fickey and Sides.)* …just so they can make a pathetic joke like that?
Eve	*(tries to get her hand back from Malcolm)* I'm afraid so.
Malcolm	*(not letting go)* Are there any more at the station like you?
Amelia	I hope to goodness not. Not with a name like Eve Nunnall…
Sides Fickey	} *(together; again)* Evenin' all.
Amelia	*(turns on them)* Will you two stop that!?
Malcolm	*(still eyeing Eve)* Dashed attractive, though, isn't she? 'Bout time we had a bit of glamour round the place. She could have the top off my boiled egg any morning.
Amelia	Will you control yourself, Malcolm! It's embarrassing! Anyone'd think you'd never seen a girl before. Let go of her hand, will you!?
Malcolm	Must I?
Amelia	Yes!

	(Malcolm lets Eve's hand go. She looks at her hand with distaste and wipes it on her skirt.)
Sides	Excuse me, Sir.., Ma'am...
Amelia	Yes, Inspector?
Sides	If we *could* get back to the murder... I'd like to ask you a few questions, if I may.
Amelia	Yes, of course, Inspector. Fire away.
	(The door R suddenly opens and the arm with the pistol appears.)
Amelia	*(calls to off R)* No, not yet. When I said "fire away" I didn't mean that...
	(The arm withdraws, returns a moment later and clicks its fingers in disappointment and closes the door.)
Amelia	*(calls to off R)* Thank you. *(To Sides)* Now, Inspector, I'm all yours. Ask your questions.
Sides	Thank you, Lady Amelia. *(Takes a notebook and pen from pocket.)* Firstly, may I ask where you were when the terrible deed was done?
Amelia	Yes, that's easy. I was in here with Sir Malcolm and Freddy.
	(Sides starts to take notes, but her pen will not write. She shakes it and tries again, without success.)
Sides	Blast! My pen's run out. Fickey, have you a pen on you?
Fickey	No, Ma'am. They only let me have wax crayons.
Eve	I've got one, Ma'am.
	(Eve lifts the hem of her skirt and pulls a pen from the top of her stocking. Sir Malcolm and Freddy cannot believe their eyes. She holds out the pen towards Sides, but Sir Malcolm takes it from her.)
Malcolm	Allow me. *(Takes pen.)* Mmmm! Still warm. *(Hands the pen to Sides.)*
Sides	Thanks, Nunnall.
Eve	You're welcome, Ma'am. Any time.
Malcolm	*(lustfully)* How about now?
Amelia	Malcolm! Will you control yourself!
Malcolm	Yes, dear. Sorry, dear.
Amelia	*(to Sides)* Look, Inspector, I don't mean to be offensive, but Eve... *(Casts a glance at Sides and Fickey and decides against saying "Eve Nunnall")* WPC Nunnall here seems to be distracting the menfolk somewhat. If my husband's tongue hangs out any farther we'll be able to use it as a hearth rug. What exactly is she here for, anyway?

Sides   You mean apart from adding a bit of glamour to an otherwise fairly dull evening?

Amelia   Exactly.

Sides   Well, she has to… well… to do all the things WPC's normally do.

Amelia   Yes, but what does a WPC normally do?

Sides   Well, she er… er… I say, Nunnall, what *do* you normally do?

Eve   Well, Ma'am. I usually do the secretarial things. You know, organising this and that, making phone calls, taking notes…

Amelia   Then will you kindly get her to do her "secretarial things" before my husband and Mr Lyons die of high blood pressure. We've had enough corpses for one day.

Sides   Certainly, Lady Amelia, good idea. Take notes, please, WPC Nunnall.

Eve   Yes, Ma'am.

            (Sir Malcolm and Freddy look towards Eve in eager anticipation as she reaches and gets another pen from her stocking, then reaches inside her blouse and pulls out a notebook. Sir Malcolm and Freddy look at each other wide-eyed, and Freddy mops his brow.)

Malcolm *(hopeful)* You wouldn't happen to have a bottle of brandy on you, m'dear?

Eve   *(weary)* No, sir.

Malcolm *(disappointed)* Shame. Would've been just the right temperature, too.

Eve   Ready, Ma'am.

Sides   Good. *(Paces the floor)* Now, Lady Amelia, Sir Malcolm and Mr Lyons were in here. Is that correct?

Amelia   Yes.

            (Eve makes notes.)

Sides   Mabel, the maid, was in the er… little room, and Smalls was…

            (There is a loud unearthly scream off R. They all look up, startled.)

Freddy   What on earth was that?

Fickey   Before you ask, Ma'am. *I'm* not going. It's *your* turn.

Sides   Nonsense, Fickey. Off you go. That's an order.

Fickey   Then you'd better give me the sack, cause I'm not going. There's something not nice out in that hall, I know there is. It's dark… and it's probably full of cobwebs…, and spiders…

Mabel   *(aside)* I don't think I want to meet the spider that made a noise like that.

Fickey   *(mocking)* Anyway, Ma'am. Surely a brave and overpaid Police Inspector like you's not afraid of a teeny-weeny inhuman scream. Take your truncheon, you'll be all right.

Sides   *(with relief)* Ah, I can't go, I haven't got a truncheon. You'll *have* to go.

Fickey   *(arms folded; stubborn)* Borrow one, then. I'm not going.

Sides   *(with a resigned sigh)* Oh alright, I'll go. Your truncheon, if you please, Nunnall.

(Sir Malcolm and Freddy very quickly turn to look at Eve with anticipatory grins on their faces.)

Fickey   *(eagerly takes out his truncheon - a baseball bat - from his jacket.)* Here, Ma'am. Use mine.

Sides   *(shocked by its size)* That's not standard issue, Fickey. Where on earth did you get it?

Fickey   *(possessive)* It's my own, Ma'am. The American model. Except *they* call them baseball bats. I bought it with vouchers.

Sides   *(puzzled)* Vouchers…?

Fickey   Yes, Ma'am. Truncheon vouchers.

Amelia   Oh, for heaven's sake…

Fickey   *(begging)* Can I use it later on, Ma'am? Can I thump someone? Please, Ma'am. That Smalls bloke'd do.

Sides   Shut up, constable.

Fickey   But Ma'am…

Malcolm   *(still stares at Eve)* Shut up, constable!

Fickey   *(turns on Malcolm; threatening)* Yer what!?

Freddy   *(also still staring)* Shut up, constable.

Fickey   *(turns on Freddy, truncheon pointed)* You can't talk to me like that. I'm…

Sides   *Fickey…!*

Fickey   *(stands to attention)* Ma'am…?

(Sides raises her foot ready to stamp on his.)

Fickey   No, Ma'am, not my corn again, please. I'll shut up. I will, Ma'am… I'm shutting up, Ma'am… See? There… I've shut up.

(Sides stamps on his foot anyway.)

Fickey   *(hops)* Ow, Ma'am! Right on it again!

Sides   Now, Nunnall, your truncheon…

(Now Sir Malcolm, Freddy and Sides all stare eagerly towards Eve, while Fickey sulks. Eve makes as if she is about to

Sides: Go and see if Smalls has anything Suitable

Eve: yes ma'am (Exit)

search about herself for her truncheon.)

Malcolm	*(starts to rise)* Need any help, Eve…?
Eve	No, thank you, Sir Malcolm. *(To Sides)* I'm sorry, Ma'am. I seem to have left it in my little Panda.

(The three men groan and look away disappointedly.)

Fickey	*(eager again) Now* can I use mine, Ma'am?
Sides	No, DC Fickey.
Fickey	*(childish)* But, Ma'am. If she hasn't got hers, why can't I use mine?
Sides	*(confidentially, to Fickey)* Look, Detective Constable, I didn't *really* want a truncheon at all. It's just that… *(Imitating Eve's previous actions when getting her pens and notebook)* …after the pens, then the notebook, everyone expected her to… *(Nods his head to indicate Eve)* Well, you know what I mean…
Fickey	*(nods his agreement, but not really understanding)* No, Ma'am.
Sides	*(defeated)* You really *do* live up to your name, don't you, Fickey?
Fickey	*(proudly)* Oh, yes, Ma'am. Very proud of my name, Ma'am. *(Rambling)* Runs in the family, you know. There've been generations of Fickies in my family. My father was a Fickey, and his father before him, and his father… They were all Fickies.
Mabel	*(aside)* I'd never have guessed it.
Sides	Well it doesn't matter. I'll go without a truncheon. Whoever or whatever it was has probably gone by now, anyway.

(The door R slowly opens and the hand appears again holding the pistol, which it points at Fickey. Amelia notices it.)

Amelia	*(points)* Look out, it's a gun!
Fickey	A what?

(Everyone except Fickey ducks for cover. Fickey moves slowly this way and that but the gun follows his every move.)

Fickey	Oh, no, not again… *(More movement; then, calling; pleading)* Inspector Sides, Ma'am.
Sides	*(from cover)* What is it, Constable?
Fickey	*(still moving)* Er… Help, Ma'am. I don't want to be shot again. It hurts like mad and it ruins my clothes.
Sides	*(gradually moves from cover)* Don't be stupid, Fickey. It's not a *real* gun. It can't hurt you.
Fickey	*(still moving and still watching the following pistol)* I don't

	mean the gun, Ma'am. It's this floor. It's covered in muck and it's ever so lumpy.
Amelia	*(also emerging from cover)* We can't just let him get shot…
Fickey	Thank you, Ma'am. I knew I could count on you…
Amelia	Not here, anyway. Think of all the trouble we had last time.
Malcolm	*(also emerging)* Yes, took us ages to get the body off stage.
Fickey	But, Sir…, Ma'am…
Freddy	*(Joins them)* Couldn't he go off into the wings and get shot out there?
Fickey	But…
Mabel	It would be a lot less fuss.
Fickey	But…
Amelia	No more fake bloodstains…
Fickey	But…
Malcolm	No body to shift…
Fickey	But…
Freddy	No more over-acting…
Fickey	But…
Malcolm	I think that's settled then. *(Starts to propel a protesting Fickey towards door R.)* Off you go, old chap.
Freddy	Yes, bye, old man. See you at curtain call.
Sides	*(with authority)* Now, wait a minute. I can't have you getting rid of one of my men just like that.
Fickey	*(relieved)* Oh, thanks, Inspector Ma'am. I knew I could count on you…
Amelia	*(to Sides)* Why? Perhaps *you'd* rather go instead?
Sides	Well, since you put it like that, I suppose he is a bit… er… how shall I put it…? *expendable.*
Fickey	No I'm not, Ma'am. I've never been expendable. Why, I… I… I don't even know what it means.
Sides	Bye-bye, Detective Constable… er… thingy.
	(Sides turns away and moves L as Amelia and Malcolm propel a still-protesting Fickey towards the door R.)
Fickey	Wait!
	(They all halt.)
Sides	What now?
Fickey	Has anyone got any sticking plasters?
	(They push him towards the door again. As Fickey nears the door, the arm holding the pistol withdraws. Amelia and Malcolm push Fickey out of the door and close it behind him.

They turn away from the door and face the others. After a silent pause, during which they all wait nervously, a single gunshot is heard off R. All flinch.)

Fickey   *(off R)* Ow! My corn!
(Several more gunshots ring out off R, rapidly at first, then slower and slower. With each one, they all flinch. Eventually silence reigns.)

Amelia   *(moves L)* Well, thank goodness that's over with...
(There is one final gunshot off R. All flinch.)

Fickey   *(off R)* Ow!

Malcolm   Dashed bad luck, that... getting bumped off twice in one play. *Dashed* bad luck. Ah, well, perhaps that means the rest of us are safe. Drinkies, anyone?

Amelia   *(pensive)* Hmmm, I wouldn't be too sure yet, my darling. We're not out of the woods yet. I still think it would be better to get this solved once and for all.

Mabel   Yes, me too. I won't feel safe until it is. I read my horoscope this morning. It said *(Grandly)* "Beware of a stranger who carries the spoken word in one hand and death in the other". Don't know what it meant. Really creepy it was.

Freddy   Mine said, "Not the best week to make long-term plans. If you have booked a holiday, cancel it and invest the money in life insurance."

Malcolm   Poppycock! *(Grabs his paper and looks for the horoscopes.)* What's you birthsign?

Freddy   Aquarius. What's yours?

Malcolm   *(looks in the paper; not hearing)* What's that, old chap?

Freddy   I said "What's yours".

Malcolm   *(looks up)* Very decent of you, old man. I'll have a brandy.

Amelia   He meant your birth sign.

Malcolm   Oh, I see... Well, I'm not certain, actually. Us Taurans don't believe in astrology... At least.. I think I'm Taurus...

Amelia   Yes, you are, my love. The sign of the newt.

Malcolm   *(corrects her)* The sign of the bull, old girl.

Amelia   *(amused)* The *what*?

Malcolm   You said...

Amelia   I *know* what I said...

Freddy   Now don't let's start bickering again.

Amelia   Quite right, Freddy. *(To Sides)* Now, Inspector, are you any nearer a solution to our problems?

Sides	*(consults her notebook)* Well, Lady Simpson-Squire…, I've considered all the evidence and reports we've so far obtained…
Amelia	*(patiently)* Yes…
Sides	…And I've examined the room where the first murder occurred…
Amelia	*(still patient)* Yes…
Sides	Of course I'll have to examine the scene of the second crime…
Amelia	Yes…
Sides	…Oh, and I've questioned everyone in the house..
Amelia	Yes…
Sides	Er…
Amelia	No, Inspector.
Sides	*(puzzled)* "No", your ladyship?
Amelia	You're not, are you…? Any nearer to solving the crimes, I mean.
Sides	Well…
Amelia	*Are* you?
Sides	*(drops her chin)* No, your ladyship.
Amelia	*(moves towards the phone)* Well, then there's nothing else for it…
Malcolm	What?
Amelia	I'm going to call… *(Dramatically)* Miss Marbles!
	(They all gasp. Amelia looks in the telephone directory. Sides looks angry and exits.)
Freddy	*(excited)* What!? Not the famous old lady who visits people's houses and someone always gets murdered while she's there and she solves the case?
Amelia	No, of course not. You're thinking of Miss Marple. This one is a little old woman who works in the post office and visits people *after* they've had a murder and then solves the case. *(Dials phone.)*
Mabel	And they always have a stupid policeman in the story who couldn't solve a crossword if he had the answers in front of him? Except we've got a police woman. *(All turn and look at Sides.)*
Amelia	Yes… that's right. She should feel right at home here. *(Into phone)* Oh, hello. I'd like to speak to Miss Marbles, please… Oh, I see… when will she be back…? Yes, could you ask her to come up to Squire Grange as soon as she can…? Yes, it

is urgent - there's been a shooting or two. Tell her if she doesn't get here fairly soon we're all sunk... Thank you... Oh, yes. I'm Lady Amelia Simpson-Squire. And you are...? Hercule Perrier. Belgian, are you...? Oh, I'm sorry, French people always sound like Belgians to me... Right, thank you Monsieur Perrier. Goodbye.

Malcolm Well...?

Amelia She's out on another case up at the Old People's Home.

Malcolm What...? Sherlock Flats?

Amelia That's the one. Apparently there's another dramatic society just like ours who have just murdered Shakespeare.., whoever he was.

Freddy When will she get here?

Amelia The chap I spoke to said she'd probably be here at the start of Act 3.

Malcolm So we'll just have to wait. *(Glances at his watch, then out of the "window".)* It's getting awfully dark. *(Calls to off L)* For heaven's sake draw the curtains before anyone else gets bumped off.

The CURTAIN falls

ACT III

As the curtain rises, Malcolm is seated in the armchair R. He is dozing over a copy of "The Times", his empty brandy glass in his hand. MABEL enters, carrying a telegram.)

Mabel 'Scuse me, Sir. *(There is no response. Louder)* Sir Malcolm... Sir!

Malcolm *(after a loud snore; comes to)* Eh..!? What!? Oh, yes, Mabel. What is it?

Mabel *(holds out the telegram)* This has arrived, Sir.

Malcolm What is it?

(Amelia enters R.)

Mabel It's a wire, Squire.

Amelia What's that, Mabel?

Mabel It's a telegram, Ma'am.

Malcolm So much for poetry.

Mabel What shall I do with it, Sir?

Malcolm Just put the cable on the table, Mabel.

Mabel   Yes, Sir.
               (MABEL puts the telegram on the table and exits L.)
Amelia   *(to Malcolm)* Aren't you going to read it?
Malcolm   No... No, not yet.
Amelia   Why? It might be important.
Malcolm   Yes, it *is*. *(Sotto voce) We* can't read it... That stupid
               Detective Constable has to read it later.
Amelia   Oh yes. Sorry... I forgot. *(After a pause)* Hold on, though,
               darling. He was murdered at the end of the last act, wasn't
               he?
Malcolm   *(puzzled)* Was he...? Wasn't that the *first* act?
Amelia   Yes, but he was somebody else then, wasn't he?
Malcolm   Was he..? Oh yes. He was that Vic Tim chappie then, wasn't
               he? That's dashed awkward. Who's going to read the
               telegram, then? I'm sure it was supposed to be him.
Amelia   Shall I go backstage and get him?
Malcolm   No, better not... I tell you what, darling. Nip off and get a copy
               of the script, will you? P'raps we can find out what's going on.
Amelia   *(sits on the settee)* I can't do that! What would *(Indicates the
               audience) they* think?
Malcolm   Perhaps we should ask that Prompt lassie. She's bound to
               know. *(To off R)* I say... Mrs Prompt... are you there?
Amelia   Malcolm! You can't...!
Prompt   Isn't it about time Miss Marbles was here?
Malcolm   *(to off R)* What's that, old girl?
Prompt   *(impatiently and more deliberately)* Isn't it about time Miss
               Marbles was here?
Malcolm   *(with realisation)* Oh, I get you... *(To Amelia)* I say, Amelia,
               darling.
Amelia   *(distracted)* Hmmm?
Malcolm   Isn't it about time Miss Marbles was here?
Amelia   Why, what time is it?
Malcolm   *(looks at his watch)* It's er... five past Act 3.
Amelia   Yes, I suppose you're right. She'd better come soon. I've got
               to be changed and home before too long.
Malcolm   What d'you mean?
Amelia   Baby-sitter, darling.
Malcolm   Oh, I see. I'll ring for Smalls and get him to gee her up a bit.
               (Shouts to off L) Smalls! Ding-a-ling! Smalls! Ding-dong! *(To
               Amelia)* I wish Props could have found us a proper bell. I feel

a right idiot doing this. *(Moves to the door L)* Smalls! Ding-a-ling!

Smalls   *(enters R. In a superior tone)* With respect, Sir Malcolm, I do not wish to be called a "dingaling".

Malcolm   *(turns)* What's that, Smalls, old chap...? Oh, I see what you mean... No, I was pretending to ring a servants' bell. The Props chappies couldn't find a real one, so...

Smalls   Oh, I see. I beg your pardon, Sir. Shall we try again?

Malcolm   Yes, if you like.

                    (Smalls exits R. Amelia rises and goes to the "window".)

Smalls   *(off R)* Ready when you are, Sir!

Malcolm   *(calls off L)* Smalls! Ding-a-ling!

Smalls   *(as he enters R)* You rang, Sir?

Malcolm   *(turns)* Ah, there you are, Smalls. Has that Marbles woman arrived yet?

Smalls   I believe not, Sir.

Amelia   *(peers out)* This fog's a bit thick. Perhaps she's lost.

Smalls   I've often thought you'd lost your marbles, Sir.

Malcolm   *(offended)* Eh!? What did you say, Smalls?

Smalls   *(cups a hand to his ear)* I said "I think that's the doorbell now, sir." *(Nothing happens. After a pause, louder)* I think that's the doorbell now, sir!

                    (The doorbell rings off R.)

Amelia   *(moves to settee)* So it is. Go and get it will you, Smalls? *(Sits.)*

Smalls   *(as he exits R)* Certainly Ma'am.

Malcolm   You really think this woman can solve the murders, Amelia?

Smalls   *(enters R carrying a doorbell.)* The doorbell, Ma'am.

Amelia   Smalls, when I said to get the doorbell, I meant answer it.

Smalls   Yes, Ma'am.

Amelia   And if you value your position within this household, you'll not try any cheap jokes like that again.

Smalls   *(sheepish)* Yes, Ma'am.

Amelia   Now go and *answer* the door.

                    (Smalls raises a finger as if to say something, then sees Amelia's icy stare thinks better of it.)

Smalls   *(turns to R)* Yes, Ma'am. *(Exits R. Off R)* Three bags full, Ma'am.

Amelia   He'll have to go. Now, where were we?

Malcolm   I was saying... You really think this woman can solve the

murders?
(Freddy enters L.)

Amelia   I should think so. I've heard very good reports of her. Oh, hello, Freddy. Come and sit down.

Freddy   *(sits by Amelia. Worried)* Thanks, Amelia. Dreadful business, all this.

Amelia   Oh, I don't know. Act One was a bit slow, but we're...

Freddy   No, I don't mean the play. I mean all these murders.

Malcolm Oh, I shouldn't worry, old man. Miss Marbles should be here at any moment. She'll sort it all out, just you see.

Freddy   You really think so?

Malcolm *(reassuring)* 'Course she will. Amelia was just saying... she's heard very good reports.

Amelia   It'll be just like on the television, Freddy. These little old ladies always get their man.

Freddy   You know, I'd hate to be friends with one of these television sleuths.

Malcolm How d'you mean, old man?

Freddy   Well, just think about it. Wherever they go... to a party, a wedding, on holiday... anywhere... somebody they know gets bumped off. I'm surprised they've any friends left.

Amelia   Yes, you have a point there. But that's television... this is real life...

Malcolm *(disbelief)* It's *what*!?
(Smalls enters R)

Amelia   Or at least it's supposed to be. I'm sure we'll be quite safe. Yes, Smalls?

Smalls   There's a body in the hall, Ma'am.

Amelia   *(shocked)* Oh my, Smalls...

Smalls   What about your *smalls*, Madam?

Amelia   Oh, so that's it. I've been wondering why you were called "Smalls" from the very beginning. And it's obviously so you could make a *ridiculous* joke about ladies' underwear.

Smalls   Of *corsets* not, Madam.

Amelia   That's enough, Smalls. Now, let's try again... You say there's a body in the hall?

Smalls   A Miss Marbles, Ma'am.

Freddy   *(jumps up)* Oh no! She's only just got here... and now you say she's dead!?

Amelia   *(calming)* Sit down, Freddy. He doesn't mean a *dead* body.

It's just his butler's way of saying "There's *some*body in the hall". Isn't that so, Smalls?

Smalls *(superior)* Very perceptive of you, Ma'am.

Freddy Oh, thank goodness for that. I thought he was trying to scare us.

Malcolm Well, yes... he was doing that, too. Show Miss Marbles in, will you, Smalls?

Smalls Very good, Sir. *(Exits R.)*

Amelia Now, Malcolm. When she comes in I want you on your best behaviour.

Malcolm *(airy)* Don't know what you mean, old girl.

Amelia I saw the way you behaved when that young policewoman was here... *(To Freddy) And* you, Freddy. I want no more of that.

Malcolm Now see here, Amelia... Miss Marbles is probably old enough to be my... my...

Amelia Twin sister?

Malcolm ...My maiden aunt. I hardly think I'm likely to... Anyway, what d'you mean "The way I behaved" with Eve... I mean the young policewoman?

Amelia Oh, don't come the innocent with me, Malcolm. I noticed the way you looked at her. Not only that, but you haven't had a drink since she got here.

Malcolm So...?

Amelia You don't fool me. You're laying off the brandy just so you can focus better.

Malcolm Nonsense! I'm just taking it easy, that's all. All these comments you and Freddy keep making...

Amelia *(points at Malcolm's stomach) And* I've noticed you holding in that thing which you used to call a waist... Here, you're not wearing that corset I bought you, are you...?

Malcolm Now, Amelia. This has gone far enough! I am not, *(To the audience)* repeat *not* wearing a corset...

Smalls *(enters R and stands just inside the door. announcing)* Miss Marbles, Ma'am, Sirs.

(Marbles enters R. She is wearing a shawl and a hat and carries an old knitting bag.)

Malcolm *(rises and moves to her)* How d'you do, Miss Marbles? My name is...

Marbles Your name is Sir Malcolm Squire. How do you do? *(Shakes hand.)*

Malcolm   And this is…

Marbles   This is your wife, Lady Amelia Simpson Squire. *(Turns towards Freddy; obviously impressed)* And this is Mr Freddy Lyons.

Malcolm   That's incredible! How on earth d'you know all that? We've never met, have we?

(Marbles continues to survey Freddy, who starts to feel uncomfortable.)

Marbles   *(still eyeing Freddy)* I make it my business to know everyone before I take a case.

Malcolm   Very wise. *(To Smalls)* Smalls, take the old bag in the other room, will you?

Amelia   Malcolm!

Marbles   *(hands Smalls her bag and shawl)* And my shawl as well, if you will, young man. Now, if you don't mind… we'll make a start.

(Smalls takes the shawl and bag and exits L.)

Malcolm   Shall I get the Police Inspector?

Marbles   What!? The Police are involved!? Oh, no. Don't tell me… Inspector Sides?

Amelia   That's right… Do you know her?

Marbles   Yes, I'm afraid so. Officious, bungling, pompous, incompetent…

Amelia   Surely she's not that bad?

Marbles   *(brusque)* Don't you believe it. Those are her good points. I can't stand the woman. *(Faces Freddy; warmly)* Now Mr Lyons here… he's different again… polite, charming, handsome… I've often admired you from afar, Mr Lyons.

Freddy   *(embarrassed)* Oh, come now, Miss Marbles, we hardly know each other…

Amelia   Are we talking about the same man… *This* Freddy Lyons?

Freddy   Now, now, Amelia, there's no need to be insulting. Miss Marbles is obviously a… lady who can appreciate the finer points in a chap's character.

Malcolm   I er… don't mean to interrupt the mutual admiration society, but shouldn't we deal with the er… emergency before we get tangled up in romantic reveries?

Marbles   *(reluctantly turns away from her admiration of Freddy)* Yes, you're right, of course, Sir Malcolm. Until later, then… Freddy.

Malcolm   Good! I'll go and get Inspector Sides.

Marbles   No, not yet if you don't mind. I'd like to get a few details clear in my mind before that woman confuses me. Please, sit down all of you.

(They all sit.)

Marbles Now first of all, how many murders have there been exactly?

Amelia *(together)* Two.
Malcolm   Three.

Marbles Now come along, please. Surely we can at least agree how many murders we've had?

Amelia Definitely two!

Malcolm It was *three!* *(To Amelia)* You remember, Amelia. First that Tim fellow was shot…

Amelia Yes…

Malcolm Then the Producer was beaten to death…

Amelia I thought he died in a car crash…

Malcolm Then there was Detective Constable Fickey…

Marbles *Defective* Constable, you mean. Don't tell me somebody's done humanity a good turn and removed Fickey from this green and pleasant land?

Malcolm That's right. Just before the end of Act Two.

Amelia But Malcolm… we can't be sure he's actually dead, can we?

Marbles I know what you mean in Fickey's case. I've a suspicion he's been dead for years, but he's been too stupid to realise it.

Malcolm But Amelia, we heard the shots… We heard him scream…

Amelia That still doesn't prove anything.

(Fickey enters L, limping, without being noticed.)

Marbles There's only one way to be sure. We'll have to examine the bodies. I'll have a look at the first one, I think… *Vic Tim*, did you say?

(Fickey looks at his costume, raises his eyebrows and turns to the door L, loosening his tie as he goes.)

Malcolm *(notices Fickey)* It'd probably be easier for everyone if you looked at the Detective Constable first.

(Fickey turns back to face them, doing up his tie again.)

Marbles *(indignant)* If you *don't* mind, Sir Malcolm, I'd like to delay seeing Fickey until I absolutely have to. It's not long since I ate.

(Fickey gives a look of frustration and turns and limps off L, once again loosening his tie as he goes.)

Amelia As you wish. You know best.

Marbles Yes, as you say… *I* know best. But then again, I suppose it would make sense to see Fickey's body while it's still fresh... *(Fickey gives an anguished cry from off L, then enters, his tie in his hand.)*

Fickey *(limps C)* Now look here, Marbles... you can't go messing people around like this. D'you want to see Fickey or the other bloke?

Amelia *(shocked to see him)* Detective Constable Fickey! We thought you'd been... I mean... what about all those shots?

Fickey Missed me by miles. One got me in the leg, *(Dramatically; as if a martyr)* but it's only a flesh wound. Whoever is doing all this shooting is a lousy aim.

Marbles Yes, you can say that again. Oh, well... it can't be helped, I suppose. Perhaps we'll be more lucky next time.

Sides *(enters R. annoyed)* Has anyone seen Detective Constable... Oh, there you are, Fickey. Where the devil have you been?

Fickey Ah, I've been looking for you, Ma'am. I've got some new evidence...

Sides *(very annoyed)* Never mind about that now, DC Fickey. Where have you been?

Fickey *(limps to her)* I've been dodging bullets, Ma'am! One got me in the leg..!

Sides *(furious)* No lame excuses, Fickey! There's work to be done. We can't have you disappearing every few minutes.

Marbles Inspector Sides. Can't you control your temper for a few minutes? Fickey here, useless though he normally is, says he has some new evidence...

Sides I'll thank you not to interrupt, Miss Marbles. This is Police business, and, much to my relief, you do not, for the present at least, have any control over the Police Force.

Marbles Yes, but surely...

Sides *(ignores her; to Fickey angrily)* I've had as much as I can stand of your complete disregard for my authority, Fickey. You're fired!

Fickey But Ma'am...

Sides Fired, Fickey... Sacked...! Given the big elbow...! The boot!

Fickey But Ma'am... I've been trying to tell you... I know who's been doing the murders.

(The door R opens and the hand with the pistol appears.)

Sides *(amazed)* You do!?

Amelia Really? Then who...?

Fickey Well, Ma'am, I was off over there and...

(Before Fickey can complete his answer, a single shot is fired and Fickey falls to the floor below C. The hand holding the pistol withdraws and the door closes.)

Freddy   Oh, no… Not again.

(Sides rushes over to Fickey's body.)

Amelia   Is he… dead?

Sides   *(sniffs the air.)* He's dead alright, and if I'm not mistaken, he's been recently fired.

Marbles   Congratulations, Inspector. You appear to have done it again.

Sides   What?

Marbles   Don't you see? He was about to reveal the name of the murderer. If you'd only let him talk all this would be over with.

Sides   Well, er… I er…

Marbles   No matter! On with the investigation. Since we no longer have any need to see Fickey's body, we'd better have a look at Vic Tim's.

(Fickey raises his head and mouths "What!?" and lets his head fall back heavily on the floor.)

Malcolm   *(looks awkwardly at Fickey)* Er… No… You can't do that.

Marbles   *(indignant)* I can and I will!

Amelia   You can't and you won't!

Marbles   Are you telling *me* - Miss Marbles - I can't see the body. How *dare* you…?

Freddy   *(rises and goes towards Miss Marbles)* No, Miss Marbles, you can't, you see, because…

(The conversation becomes inaudible as Freddy whispers in Miss Marbles' ear, animatedly pointing as he does so at Fickey's body and off stage L and R, and making wild gesticulations of guns shooting, strangling, stabbing and bodies falling. Sides shakes her head and exits L.)

Marbles   *(after he has finished)* Ah, I see. Well, if *you* say so, Mr Lyons…

Freddy   *(politely)* Freddy, please.

Marbles   *(like a star-struck little girl)* If you say so… Freddy… then it's alright.

(Fickey raises his head and rubs the back of it, then reaches over to the settee, gets a cushion and places it under his head and plays dead again.)

Malcolm   *(a sudden idea)* I know, Miss Marbles. You can look at his body in the wings… *(Quickly)* I mean the study. Freddy, take Miss Marbles into the study.

Freddy   *(to Malcolm: sotto voce)* The where?

Malcolm   The study... You know... *(Indicates off L with a crooked thumb.)* The *study*!

Freddy   *(realises)* Oh, I see. The *study*. Right. *(Turns to go, then turns back to Malcolm.)* Wait a minute, Malcolm. You don't expect me to go in there..? Alone?

    (Marbles moves towards the door L.)

Malcolm   Don't be scared, old man. You'll be alright. It's only a body. Anyway, I think Miss Marbles likes you.

Freddy   Yes, that's what I'm afraid of. The body doesn't bother me a bit.

Malcolm   Go on, old man. You'll be OK.

Freddy   *(reluctantly)* Well, alright... But if you hear me scream, promise you'll come running.

Marbles   *(takes Freddy's tie and pulls him L)* Come along... Freddy. Come with Ermintrude.

Freddy   *(to Malcolm; choking)* Ermintrude!? Malcolm... promise.

Malcolm   *(amused)* You have my word as a gentleman, old chap.

Freddy   *(not comforted)* Oh, great!

    (Marbles drags Freddy off L.)

Amelia   What a to-do. A bumbling old dragon, bodies all over the place and an incompetent Inspector who is, to say the least, a few sandwiches short of a picnic.

Malcolm   Never mind, old girl. I'm sure they'll all have it sorted out before too long.

Amelia   I hope you're right. I know I said I was bored out here, but I'd give an awful lot for a bit of good old boredom right now.

    (Amelia and Malcolm sit and look bored.)

Malcolm   Fancy a drink, Amelia?

Amelia   No, not really. Too early for me. You can have one if you want.

Malcolm   Yes, I was going to. *(Calls off R)* Smalls!

Smalls   *(enters L.)* Sir?

Malcolm   I know it's a bit early in the day, Smalls, and we don't er... normally do this sort of thing, but in the circumstances...

Smalls   Your *regular* afternoon brandy coming right up, Sir. *(Exits L.)*

Malcolm   We'll have to get a new butler, you know. He acts way above his position.

Smalls   *(Off L)* Well, at least *I* act.

Malcolm   *(calls to off L)* And make sure it *is* brandy this time. *(To*

Amelia) Any more cold tea and I'm leaving.

Amelia   *(not really hearing)* Mmmm…? *(Rises impatiently)* Oh, why doesn't something happen?

Malcolm   Careful what you're saying, Amelia, old girl. You said that at the start of the play… when I was pretending to be asleep. Then look what happened.

Amelia   Yes… Don't remind me. I somehow feel responsible for all these murders.

Fickey   *(raises his head again; to Amelia; threatening)* So, you admit it, eh? I knew it was you all along…

Amelia   *(to Fickey)* Shut up you…! You're dead.

Fickey   Oh, yes… I forgot. Sorry. *(To audience)* Sorry. *(Plays dead again.)*

Amelia   *(sobs into Malcolm's shoulder)* Oh, Malcolm, what have I done?

Malcolm   *(comforts her)* Now, Amelia, you mustn't feel responsible. It wasn't your fault. *You* didn't write the script…

(Fickey raises his head again and tries to beckon to Amelia, who notices but ignores him. With increasing urgency he continues to try to attract her attention through the following dialogue.)

Amelia   If I hadn't gone on so about finding a plot for my new novel perhaps none of this would've happened.

Malcolm   You don't know that. It might have just been coincidence.

Amelia   Oh, I wish I could believe that. What a waste of life! Poor Mr Tim… The Producer… And then Detective Constable Fickey…

(Fickey is now getting very agitated. He grabs Amelia's foot.)

Malcolm   *(aside)* Well, two out of three isn't bad.

Amelia   *(dramatically)* …Cut down in the prime of his life. *(Sotto voce to Fickey; trying to get her foot back but losing her shoe in the process; annoyed)* What is it?

(Fickey beckons to Amelia, and she goes and bends to him. A whispered conversation takes place, with Amelia shaking her head several times and Fickey pleading. Amelia takes her shoe back from Fickey.)

Amelia   *(chiding)* You'll have to wait. You should have gone in the interval. *(Puts her shoe back on.)*

Malcolm   *(stands; to Amelia; sotto voce)* What's the matter?

Amelia   *(indicates Fickey)* It's him. He wants the er… *(Indicates off R.)*

(Fickey is now clearly uncomfortable.)

Malcolm He can't!

Amelia That's what I told him. He says he's desperate!

Malcolm But he can't just walk off. He's supposed to have been shot.
(Fickey attempts to get up. Malcolm and Amelia each put a foot on him to restrain him.)

Amelia *(points to the settee)* Perhaps if we…

Malcolm No! Definitely not! I am *not* doing that stupid bit with the sofa again.

Amelia Well, we'll have to do something. The poor chap's in pain.

Malcolm *(after a sigh)* Any suggestions?

Amelia Let me think… *(She has an idea.)* I know. *(Suddenly; points at Fickey)* Malcolm!

Malcolm *(jumps; shocked)* What!?

Amelia *(points)* Look! DC Fickey!

Malcolm *(sotto voce)* Amelia, what the devil are you doing? This isn't in the script.

Amelia *(sotto voce)* I know… I'm ad-libbing.

Malcolm *(sotto voce)* Are we allowed to do that?

Amelia I don't know.

Malcolm What will the Producer say?

Amelia *(sotto voce)* He's dead, remember? Never mind that… just join in.

Malcolm *(sotto voce)* Alright. I'll try. Carry on.

Amelia *(points at Fickey again)* Look! He moved!
(They remove their restraining feet. Fickey wriggles. They replace their feet on him and he stops.)

Malcolm By Jove, you're right!

Amelia Perhaps he was only wounded.
(They remove their feet from Fickey and help him up. He stands and fidgets.)

Malcolm You alright, old man?

Fickey Er… Yes, I think so. It er… must have been another flesh wound. *(Agitated)* Can I go, now?

Amelia Yes, you can go.
(Fickey starts to shuffle off R, legs held together.)

Malcolm *(thoughtful)* Detective Constable Fickey…

Fickey *(impatient; in anguish)* What…? What is it?

Malcolm This flesh wound of yours…

Fickey   What about it?

Malcolm   You'd better make sure it causes amnesia.

Fickey   Don't be silly. I never have any trouble getting to sleep.

Amelia   He said "amnesia", not "insomnia". It means loss of memory.

Fickey   Oh, yes. I forgot.
              (Smalls enters L carrying a brandy glass on a tray.)

Malcolm   You were about to reveal the name of the murderer when you
              were shot. If you're suddenly magically alive again, we can't
              have you spilling the beans or the whole play'll be over in five
              minutes.

Smalls   Not a moment too soon, if I may say so, Ma'am.

Amelia   *(takes brandy from tray)* No, you may not, Smalls. That is all.

Smalls   Yes, Ma'am. *(Exits L.)*
              *(As Malcolm holds out his hand for the brandy, Amelia sits
              and unthinkingly drinks it. Malcolm looks on disappointed.
              Fickey, sensing a suitable point to depart, rushes off R, trying
              to limp and waddle at the same time.)*

Amelia   *(stands; hands Malcolm the glass)* I can't stand all this waiting
              around. I'm going to see what Miss Marbles and Freddy are
              up to.

Malcolm   I'm sure Freddy will be most relieved. *(Rises)* I'll follow you
              shortly... after I've had my brandy. *(Calls to off R)* Smalls!

Amelia   *(moves L)* Not another one. Don't you ever stop?
              (Amelia exits L just as Eve enters R.)

Malcolm   *(looks L)* But...!

Eve   *(sees Malcolm)* Oh, sorry, Sir. I didn't know you were in here.
              Shall I come back later? (stand in doorway)

Malcolm   *(visibly and obviously stands upright, pulls in his stomach,
              and pulls back his chest and shoulders)* No, please. It's no
              bother. Come on in. Anything I can do for you?
              *(Eve looks half-heartedly round the room. Malcolm follows
              her every move with lecherous interest.)* — Don't move

Eve   Inspector Sides has asked me to have another look around
              the room. Says a young pair of eyes might spot something
              they missed. — Look under cushions on settee

Malcolm   From what I've seen of those two so far, the culprit could
              hand them a confession in four-foot high neon letters and
              they'd still miss it.

Eve   *(with a smile)* They're not that bad really. Move to window
              (Eve has arrived by the "window" below C.)

Eve   *(looks out; dreamy)* Oh, I love it here... Just look at that view.

Malcolm	*(behind Eve; studies her)* Yes… I am looking.
Eve	*(with a sigh)* Beautiful.
Malcolm	*(with a sigh)* Beautiful.
Eve	It fills me with a sense of wonder… a primitive feeling of a *need* to be at one with nature.
Malcolm	Yes… Me too.
Eve	*(wistful pause; then back to her searching)* Ah, well… Back to reality.
Malcolm	Er… WPC Nunnall… Eve…
Eve	*(still searching)* Sir?
Malcolm	*(follows her)* Er… Look… I'll be coming into town next week. What say… er… in the evening… you and I… er…
Eve	*(faces him)* I'm sorry, Sir. I'm washing my hair that night.
Malcolm	*(taken aback)* How d'you know? I haven't even said which night, yet.
Eve	*(patiently)* Well, er… My hair gets very dirty, Sir. I wash it *every* night.
Malcolm	Must put quite a damper on your social life.
	(Freddy enters L and sits on the settee. He is very agitated.)
Eve	Yes, Sir. *(Turns and resumes her search.)*
Malcolm	How about during the day, then?
Eve	Not while I'm on duty, Sir.
Malcolm	Your day off, then?
Eve	*(stops and faces him again)* My, my, sir. We *are* being persistent today, aren't we?
Malcolm	Chap has to try, old girl.
Eve	Does he now? Look, Sir, I've tried to be polite, I've tried diplomacy. Perhaps I should try a few home truths. *You* are a married man, Sir.
Malcolm	Yes.
Eve	You have children who are older than I am.
Malcolm	Yes. I have shirts older than you are.
Eve	I am a policewoman, Sir… a *young* policewoman.
Malcolm	Yes.
Eve	I have friends my own age.
Malcolm	Yes.
Eve	With respect, Sir, I *don't* want to be harassed by you.
Malcolm	Does that mean "No"?
Eve	Yes, Sir. That is "No, Sir". It *does* mean "No".

Malcolm   Definitely and absolutely no?

Eve   Definitely and absolutely no!

Malcolm   Oh. *(Pause)* How about the week after, then?

Eve   *(aside)* So much for politeness, diplomacy and home truths. *(To Malcolm; as if addressing a child)* Let's try another tack, sir. If you don't stop your... your... advances, *Sir*, I shall be forced to inform Lady Simpson-Squire. Then I shall go and get my nice little policewoman's truncheon from my nice little blue policewoman's Panda car, bring it in here and make you several inches shorter. Now leave me alone...! Sir. *(As she exits R; calling)* Inspector Sides, Ma'am...

Freddy   *(shocked)* Malcolm...!

Malcolm   *(rubs hands together)* I love it when they play hard to get.

Freddy   What would Amelia say?

Malcolm   What about, old man?

Freddy   If she saw the way you were coming on to that girl.

Malcolm   She wouldn't say anything. She trusts me.

Freddy   Trusts you!? I never knew there was insanity in the family.

Malcolm   She's says I'm all talk. She thinks... she *knows* I wouldn't really *do* anything.

Freddy   *(distracted)* I hope you're right. She'd kill you if you tried anything on and she found out.

Malcolm   Kill me, eh? Unfortunate turn of phrase, that, Freddy, after everything that's happened here today.

Freddy   *(his mind elsewhere)* What...!? Oh, yes, perhaps you're right there. Sorry, Malcolm. *(Looks very down-at-heart.)*

Malcolm   Never mind, old man. Cheer up, it might never happen.

Freddy   *(glum)* Don't tempt fate. I'm beginning to wish I'd never come here today. First there's a murderer on the rampage, then there's the police crawling all over the place...

Malcolm   *(his mind also elsewhere)* Yes... That WPC's an attractive little thing, isn't she?

Freddy   Can't say as I've noticed.

Malcolm   Oh, come on, you can't fool me, Freddy. I've known you too long. I've seen you having a crafty ogle when you think no-one's looking.

Freddy   Never mind that... What about Miss Marbles in there?

Malcolm   *(amused)* You mean "Ermintrude"... I think you could strike lucky there, Freddy, my boy.

Freddy   *(still glum)* Why... is she leaving?

Malcolm   She's obviously got a soft spot for you.

Freddy   She's got soft spots everywhere… inside and out. From her head to her toes. Enormous ones.

Malcolm   I still think she fancies you, old man. 'Bout time you thought about settling down… taking a wife.

Freddy   Ugh! Don't be disgusting, Malcolm. What a horrific thought.

Malcolm   You could do worse, you know.

Freddy   Where? How?

Malcolm   I bet she's a terrific cook.

Freddy   Maybe…, but every time I looked at her I'd lose my appetite. And she's so… boring.

Malcolm   You know what they say, old boy… "Still waters run deep"…

Freddy   Yes… and *very* cold.

Malcolm   But just imagine it, Freddy… All those crimes she gets called to…all the excitement… pitting your wits against the best criminal minds in the country.

Freddy   I had quite enough of pitting my wits against the best criminal minds in the country when I was on the Parish Council, thank you very much. Anyway, just think about it… running around with the Medusa in there… wouldn't exactly prolong your life expectancy, would it?

Malcolm   *She's* still alive.

Freddy   You sure?

Malcolm   Imagine if *she* got a flesh wound.

Freddy   She'd need major surgery.

Malcolm   Cheer up, old man. It'll all be over soon.

Freddy   Will you stop using that sort of line? It sounds very… final, somehow. *(Stands)* Anyway, Miss Marbles says she wants us in the study.

Malcolm   *(follows Freddy to exit L)* You know, Freddy, when she came in before she reminded me of that film.

Freddy   What, one of the "Miss Marple" ones?

Malcolm   *(as they exit)* No… The Bruce Lee one… "Enter the Dragon". *(Malcolm and Freddy exit L. Eve and Sides enter R.)*

Eve   *(as she enters)* …you'd think a man his age would behave more like a gentleman.

Sides   Oh, well he's not here, now. Good. Alone at last…

Eve   That's what *he* said. I've had about as much as I can stand of that old lecher.

Sides   But he's a married man.

Eve	So?
Sides	Anyway, we haven't got time to worry about that sort of thing. I just want to get this case solved before anyone else gets bumped off. And it's even more urgent now that interfering old ratbag Miss Marbles is here. I refuse to have her make fools out of us again.
Eve	Right, Ma'am. What do you want me to do?
Sides	I have a plan. I want to set a trap… with you as the bait.
Eve	I'm going off this plan already, and I haven't even heard it yet.
Sides	You'll be perfectly safe. I'll be here with you… Except… *(Pauses.)*
Eve	*(dubious)* Except what?
Sides	Well, I was planning to get them all in here and announce that you had discovered who the killer is…
Eve	Oh, no! That's it! Count me out.
Sides	Wait a minute. You haven't heard the rest of the plan yet.
Eve	No. And I don't want to.
Sides	I'll tell them you are going to reveal the killer's name, then turn the lights out for a few moments. With any luck the killer will attempt to… er… *(Makes as if she is about to strangle Eve.)*
Eve	*(slaps Sides' hands away)* No he won't… Because *I* won't be here.
Sides	But WPC Nunnall… Eve… I've *told* you… You'll come to no harm. I'll be here to protect you.
Eve	You will…? Then who'll be turning out the lights? *(Fickey enters L, unseen by Sides and Eve.)*
Sides	*(pensive)* Oh, yes, I didn't think of that. *(After a sigh)* Oh, if only Fickey was here. *(Fickey beams.)*
Sides	*(realises what she has just said)* What am I saying?
Fickey	Never realised you cared, Ma'am. *(Eve and Sides turn to face Fickey.)*
Sides	*(amazed)* Fickey! What the…? You were shot. We saw you.
Fickey	It's alright, Ma'am. It was only insomnia.
Eve	*(puzzled)* What?
Sides	Fickey!! It's really great that you're OK…! *(Composes herself)* Well, that is to say… Ahem! Good to have you back, DC Fickey.
Fickey	Good to be back, Ma'am. *(Rubs his bottom)* Bit hard, that

	floor.
Sides	Now you're back you can help us with my plan.
Eve	But Ma'am…
Sides	*(irritated)* What now, Nunnall? I can stay with you now Fickey's back.
Eve	But you won't need to. Fickey knows who the murderer is. He was just about to reveal the name when he was shot.
Sides	Was he..? Yes, that's right. Come on, Detective Constable. Spill the beans.
Fickey	Yes, Ma'am. Certainly, Ma'am. *(Grandly)* The killer is…

(Fickey is just about to reveal the name when Amelia pokes her head through the door L and gives a loud cough. Fickey notices her, but Eve and Sides do not. Amelia holds her finger to her lips for silence, then withdraws.)

Sides	*(waits)* Well?
Fickey	I forget.
Eve	You *forget*!?
Sides	*(incredulous)* How can you forget something as important as that?
Fickey	It must have been when I was shot, Ma'am. I think the bullet must have gone right through my brain.
Eve	Must have been a *remarkably* good shot.
Fickey	*(puzzled)* Eh!?
Eve	It must have been a *very* small calibre.
Fickey	*(reacts)* You what!?
Eve	I said it was a small bore.
Fickey	*(advances on her)* Who're you calling a bore?
Eve	If the cap fits…

(Eve stamps on Fickey's foot, causing him to hop around yet again.)

Sides	*(intervenes)* Now, now, children. No fighting. We have work to do.
Fickey	Well tell her to stop picking on me.
Sides	I was telling WPC Nunnall about my plan.
Eve	Oh… I was hoping you'd forgotten.
Sides	Now, in a few minutes I'm going to call everyone in here. *(To Fickey)* You go off and find the main power switch. All right?
Fickey	Main power switch, yes.
Sides	When you hear me say "Now, Nunnall, reveal the name of the killer", I want you to turn off the power.

Fickey	Got it.
Sides	Then I want you to count to five…
Eve	Can he count that far?
Sides	*(ignores her)* …Count to five and switch it back on again. Have you got that?
Fickey	Yes, Ma'am. Got it.
Sides	And no mistakes, Fickey. Nunnall's life may depend upon you.
Eve	Have you got a Will form on you, Ma'am?
Sides	Now, do you know where the main switch is?
Fickey	Yes, Ma'am. *(Indicates the door R)* It's just outside that door and round to the right.
Sides	Good. *(After a pause)* DC Fickey…
Fickey	Yes, Ma'am?
Sides	You *can* count to five, can't you?
Fickey	Course I can, Ma'am. It's easy. *(Holds out his hand and demonstrates)* Four fingers and a thumb.
Eve	Can I telephone my mother and say goodbye first?
Sides	No, you can't! Right, Fickey, off you go. And don't forget to switch off the lights when I say the words.
Fickey	Yes, Ma'am. I won't forget. *(Exits R, then immediately pokes his head back through the door.)* What words?
Sides	"Now, Nunnall, reveal the name of the killer."
Fickey	*(puzzled)* Does she know?
Sides	Of course not! It's a trap.
Fickey	*(obviously not understanding)* A Trap. Right. Got it. *(Exits.)*
Eve	Are you *sure* there's no other way?
Sides	Courage, Nunnall, courage. Now, go and call everyone in, will you?
Eve	*(sigh)* Yes, Ma'am. *(Goes to the door L, open it and calls)* Can we have everyone in here, please? Inspector Sides has an important announcement to make. *(Comes back to L of Sides.)*
Sides	Well, done, Nunnall.
	(Everyone gradually enters L and sit as convenient. Malcolm carries his newspaper, open at the crossword, and remains standing.)
Marbles	I hope, Inspector, that this is not one of your usual pranks.
Sides	Patience, please, Miss Marbles. All will be revealed in a short while.

Malcolm   *(a lecherous look at Eve)* Oooh, goody! *(Rubs hands together.)*

Freddy   Have you discovered the culprit, Inspector?

Sides   I am pleased to say that we have. Due to painstaking and thorough police work, we have narrowed down the list of suspects to just one. WPC Nunnall, your notes, please.
(Malcolm and Freddy beam and turn to watch Eve retrieve her notebook once again.)

Eve   Got it, Ma'am.

Malcolm   *(to Eve)* Don't you need a pen..., or a typewriter or something?

Sides   Your attention, please, Sir Malcolm! Right, Nunnall. *(Grandly)* Tell them who it is. *(Looks around surprised as the lights stay on.)*

Eve   *(pointedly)* Pardon, Ma'am?

Sides   *(slowly and deliberately, glances off R)* Tell - them - who - it - is.

Eve   *(sotto voce)* The words, Ma'am.

Sides   Words? Nunnall, what are you...?

Eve   *(patiently)* "Now, Nunnall, reveal the name of the killer."

Sides   Oh, yes... *(Dramatically)* "Now, Nunnall, reveal..."
(The lights black out. There is general shuffling round on stage.)

Fickey   *(off R; slowly)* One... Two... Three... er... Four...
(Eve lets out a loud scream.)

Fickey   Er...

Sides   *(calls to off R)* Five!
(The lights come up. Malcolm is standing next to Eve, who gives him a resounding slap on the face and smooths down her skirt.)

Malcolm   *(embarrassed)* I was just... er... looking for a pencil. *(Picks up his newspaper)* For my crossword.

Amelia   Yes. He was trying to get one across.

Fickey   *(enters R in a rush.)* Did you get him? Want me to bash him for you?

Eve   Down, boy. We didn't get anyone.

Sides   What kept you, Fickey?

Fickey   I dropped my policeman's torch, Ma'am.

Marbles   Another idea bungled, eh, Sides?

Eve   Don't knock it. At least *I'm* still in one piece.

Malcolm   And a very nice piece it is, too... Don't you think, Freddy?

Freddy   I'll say!

Marbles   *(to Freddy)* I'll never understand you men. What's she got that I haven't?

Freddy   *(embarrassed)* Well, nothing, I suppose...

Malcolm   *(amused)* It's just that you've got so much *more* of it than she has... ~~Move to back wall near (SR) door~~

Freddy   *(trying not to laugh)* And hers doesn't need ironing!

Marbles   Well, really! I'm not staying here to be insulted! *(Makes to exit R.)*

Malcolm   Why? Where do you usually go?
              (Malcolm and Freddy are desperately trying not to laugh.)

Amelia   *(stops Miss Marbles)* Now, Miss Marbles. They don't mean it. They're just having a bit of fun.
              (Amelia glares at Malcolm and Freddy, who just laugh all the more.)

Marbles   Not on my account they're not! If you don't need me, I'll go.

Amelia   But we *do* need you.

Marbles   *(indicates Malcolm and Freddy)* They don't.

Amelia   Of course they do. Don't you? *(Glares at Malcolm and Freddy.)*

Malcolm   Do we?

Amelia   *(with meaning)* We do if we don't want to be the next one murdered, don't we?
              (Malcolm and Freddy sober up considerably.)

Marbles   I'll only stay if he asks me to.
              (Amelia indicates for Malcolm to ask by giving him a kick on the foot.)

Malcolm   Ouch! *(With a glare at Amelia)* Miss Marbles, I apologise. I didn't mean...

Marbles   *(to Amelia)* I didn't mean *(with disgust)* him. I meant *(tenderly)* him.

Amelia   Well, Freddy?

Freddy   *(nervously; to Miss Marbles)* Miss Marbles... Ermintrude. I would consider it a great favour if you could stay.

Marbles   *(coyly)* Say "please".
              (Malcolm splutters with suppressed laughter.)

Freddy   *(a sigh)* Please.

Marbles   *(childishly)* Shan't! So there!

Amelia   Please, Miss Marbles. We can't stay here if we don't find the

	murderer. After the little episode we've just witnessed you're our only hope. We're desperate.
Marbles	*(after some consideration)* Well, very well. But no more insults.
Amelia	No more insults. *(To Malcolm and Freddy)* No more insults!
Marbles	Very well. Now, let me see. Is everyone here?
Mabel	Apart from Fickey, yes.
Fickey	*(takes a step towards her)* Now look, you. I've told you before...
Marbles	Inspector! Will you kindly put him back in his box so we can get on?
Sides	*(patiently)* Fickey...
Fickey	Ma'am?
Sides	You know you were dead a few minutes ago?
Fickey	Yes, Ma'am.
Sides	Have you any desire to be dead again?
Fickey	No, Ma'am.
Sides	*(suddenly shouts)* Then belt up!
Fickey	Yes, Ma'am.
Marbles	Thank you, Inspector. Now, everyone is here, so we must assume, for the moment at least, that the killer is also here. Now, Inspector...
Sides	Yes, Ma'am?
Marbles	Miss!
Sides	Sorry. Yes, Miss Marbles?
Marbles	Correct me if I am wrong, but everyone in this room has established an alibi.
Sides	That is correct.
Marbles	So we must assume that either (a) everyone is in collusion...
	(All dramatically gasp at the suggestion.)
Marbles	...or (b) the guilty party is not present.
	(All dramatically gasp again.)
Marbles	Am I correct?
Sides	Well, yes. I suppose you are.
Marbles	I think it would be safe to assume that this many people could not avoid some minor slip-ups, or discrepancies in their alibis. Correct?
Sides	Yes, I suppose you're right. All their alibis agree.
Marbles	Then nobody could have done it.
Sides	What!?

move infront of fireplace (then back to (SR) door

Eve	That's silly, *someone* must have. ~~Steps infront~~
	(Fickey goes towards the audience and looks accusingly.)
Marbles	I agree. Now, let's see…
Fickey	*(points at a member of the audience, preferably an older child)* I think it was *him*, Ma'am. Always thought he looked a bit shifty from when we started. Want me to go down and extract a confession, Ma'am? *(Thumps his fist and leans towards the selected child.)*
Sides	DC Fickey! I've told you before… curb your violent inclinations.
Fickey	*(turns)* Eh? What?
Sides	Shut up, constable.
Fickey	*(turns to his "suspect" again)* I still think…
All	*Shut up,* Constable!
	(Sides stamps on Fickey's foot again.)
Fickey	*(hops up and down)* Ow, Ma'am! You got my corn again! Couldn't you get the other foot just once?
	(In the lines that follow, Fickey continues to make threatening gestures towards his "suspect", while limping on his injured foot.)
Marbles	Now, where were we?
Amelia	Trying to find the culprit.
Malcolm	Even though nobody could have done it.
Marbles	Er, yes. *(Pensive)* Now, it would have to be someone who was outside that door at the time. *(Points R.)* That's where the shots came from, isn't that so?
Sides	Yes. Every time.
Marbles	*(to Sides)* You're sure you have them *all* here?
Sides	Yes. *(Moves R; gets a programme from the wings.)* Look at the cast list in the programme if you don't believe me. They're all here.
Marbles	*(reads the programme)* Except one.
Sides	What!?
Marbles	*(suddenly reaches a conclusion)* Detective Constable Fickey…
	(Fickey is still threatening his suspect and does not hear.)
Marbles	*Detective Constable Fickey!*
Fickey	*(snaps to attention)* Yes, Sir…!? I mean yes, Mrs Sir.
Marbles	Miss! *(Indicates the door R)* Go and look outside that door. Outside you will find the culprit.

Fickey	But, Ma'am… Miss, it was *him*, I know it was. Let me go down there and drag him up here and we can beat a confession out of him.
Marbles	Detective Constable! It was *not* him… Nor any other member of the audience.
Fickey	*(doubtful)* You sure, Ma'am?
Marbles	Just think about it for a moment. We did this play *last* night and *(Points at the "suspect")* he wasn't even here then.
Fickey	*(sulky)* No, Sir… Ma'am… Miss.
Marbles	*(points to door R)* Now, will you *please* go to that door and bring in *(Dramatically)* the murderer.
Fickey	*(moves R)* Yes, Ma'am. *Open door for Fickey*
	(Fickey goes to the door R and opens it. He steps outside and drags in struggling PROMPT, who is holding a copy of the script in her left hand and the pistol in her right hand. Her right arm wears a black sleeve and black glove.)
Marbles	There you are… the culprit! *Then close door and move (DSR) infront of bookcase*
Amelia	But who *is* she?
Marbles	She's the prompt, of course.
Malcolm	Who?
Marbles	The prompt. That little voice you've been hearing every time you forgot one of your lines.
Amelia	You know, my love… the one who's been going steadily more hoarse as the evening's dragged on.
Fickey	Oh… Is that what it was…? I thought you had noisy neighbours.
Marbles	*(points) She* is the murderess.
Freddy	But how do you work that out?
Marbles	She was the only one who was in the right position at the right time. She has the murder weapon in her hand…
Mabel	Here! My horoscope said that… "Beware of a stranger who carries the spoken word in one hand and death in the other". That must've been what it meant!
Marbles	*And* she has the perfect motive.
Malcolm	What motive?
Marbles	Look… if you'd had to sit through this lot in a dark and cramped corner in the wings all evening, *you*'d want to shoot someone, wouldn't you?
Malcolm	Ah, yes… I see your point.
Prompt	*(breaks down)* All right! I did it…! I'm sorry. I didn't mean to

	do it. I've had some problems, you see. First my tortoise died - he was hibernating for the winter and when I took him his early Summer cup of tea he was… he was…
Malcolm	*(comforts her)* Steady, old girl. Steady.
Prompt	His shell was empty. He wasn't in.
Fickey	*(trying to be helpful)* Perhaps he's gone on holiday.
Prompt	Then I had awful trouble getting here. My little moped wouldn't start. Something was blocking the fuel line.
Fickey	Probably the inside of your tortoise.
Prompt	*(still tearful)* Shut up, Constable! And then I've had to sit in that little corner there all night long. It's a thankless job. Every time one of you forgot a line, there I was.
Amelia	We know… We're very grateful.
Prompt	*(angry)* You never said thanks, though, did you? Not once! So I'm *glad* I did it! You deserved it… all of you!
Freddy	Congratulations, Miss Marbles. I'd never have guessed.
Prompt	*(frees herself from Fickey's grasp and points the pistol at them.)* So you've caught me! But it won't do you any good.
Fickey	*(takes step towards her)* Now, Miss, are you going to come quietly?
Prompt	No, I'm certainly not. Not in *this* play.
	(Prompt points the pistol at Fickey. Everybody except Fickey and Sides ducks. Fickey looks round, sees everyone crouched, turns back to Prompt and ducks himself. Prompt aims at Sides and fires the pistol, but nothing happens except a dull click. She fires again and again, but it is empty.)
Sides	*(in a superior fashion)* That's a Smith and Wesson Automatic…, and you've had your two hundred and thirty-seven.
	(Fickey leaps up, grabs the gun and restrains Prompt.)
Sides	*(formal)* Mrs Prompt, you have been found in possession of the murder weapon, and by your own words you have admitted the crime. I am therefore arresting… *(Forgets her words.)* I am arresting… er… erm… I am arresting… er…
Prompt	*(realises Sides has forgotten her lines; reads from script)* I am arresting Freddy Lyons for murder…
Sides	*(copies)* I am arresting Freddy Lyons for murder.
Freddy	*(shocked)* What? But I didn't do it!
Prompt	*(reads)* Take him away, DC Fickey.
Sides	*(repeats)* Take him away, DC Fickey.
	(Fickey leads a protesting Freddy R. The rest look

questioningly and uneasily at one another.)

Marbles   Don't worry, Freddy. I'll save you.

Freddy   *(stops struggling and looks at Marbles).* Take me away, DC Fickey.

Malcolm   *(calls to off R)* Bye, Freddy. Don't forget to write.

Marbles   And he seemed such a nice man.

Malcolm   *(to Prompt)* Is that it?

Prompt   *(looks at script)* Yes. That seems to be the end.

Amelia   Just like that?

Prompt   *(turns a page)* Yes. that's the last page. *(Shows script.)* Look.

Malcolm   A bit of a sudden ending, isn't it?

Prompt   Don't blame me. I didn't write it.

(A black-sleeved and gloved arm appears once again through the door R and points the gun at Fickey.)

Amelia   *(notices gun)* Er... Mrs Prompt...

Prompt   Yes?

Amelia   *(watches gun nervously)* It *was* you who was doing all the shooting, wasn't it?

Prompt   I'm saying nothing till the police go.

Amelia   You must tell me. It's very important.

Prompt   Well, alright... Yes, it was me.

Amelia   *(points to the arm)* Then who's that?

(They all turn where she is pointing, notice the gun and gasp.)

Blackout

(A series of gunshots, then silence. Curtain.)

Fickey   *(from behind the closed curtain)* Ow! My corn!

(At the first curtain call, the cast are strewn around the furniture as if they have all been shot.)

Furniture & Property list
Throughout the play:-

On Stage	Two-seater settee
	Armchair
	Small table *(next to armchair)*
	Sideboard *(above L)*
	On it: Telephone
	Telephone Directory

ACT I

	Brandy glass *(Malcolm - nearly empty)*
	The "Times" *(Malcolm)*
	Jotter *(Amelia)*
	Box of chocolates *(Amelia)*
	Pen *(Amelia)*
Off Stage R	Business Card *(Amelia)*
	Pistol *(Prompt)*
Off Stage L	Tea Towel *(Mabel)*
	Personal
	Wristwatch *(Malcolm)*
	Wristwatch *(Amelia)*
	Sign "HELLO MUM" *(Vic)*
	Comb Malcolm - in his pocket

ACT II

On Stage	As ACT I. Malcolm's "Times", still open at the crossword *(which is part completed)* is in the armchair. An empty brandy glass is on the table.
Personal	Pistol *(Prompt)*
	Business Card *(Sides)*
	Notebook *(Fickey - in his pocket)*
	Business Card *(Fickey)*
	Notebook *(Sides - in his pocket)*
	Pen *(Sides - in his pocket)*
	Two Pens *(Eve - in her stocking)*
	Notebook *(Eve - in her blouse)*
	Baseball bat *(Fickey)*

ACT III

On Stage	As ACT I.
	The "Times" *(Malcolm)*
Off Stage R	Doorbell *(Smalls)*

Personal	Telegram *(Mabel)*
	Wristwatch *(Malcolm)*
	Knitting bag *(Miss Marbles)*
	Hat *(Miss Marbles)*
	Tray *(Smalls)*
	On it: Glass of brandy
	Notebook *(Eve - in her blouse)*
	Script *(Prompt)*
	Pistol *(Prompt)*
	Pistol *(Off Stage R)*

Effects
ACT I

● Doorbell *(Off R)*

Cue: **Amelia** Yes, me too. Still, I'm sure we'll find out before too long.

● Loud thunderclap

Cue: **Malcolm** Like a murder, for instance…

● Repeated pistol fire (from on-stage pistol)

Cue: **Vic** …Then I open the door again and come in… and move to the centre of the stage…

● Single pistol shot (from on-stage pistol)

Cue: **Malcolm** Come on, you lot. Show a bit of appreciation.

ACT II

● Single pistol shot

Cue: **Mabel** Yes, Ma'am. After he was shot. Came running back into the dressing room going on about changing into a policeman.

● Doorbell ring *(Off R)*

Cue: **Malcolm** Now look here, Amelia…

● Crash *(Off R)*

Cue: **Sides** Mabel, the maid, was in the er… little room, and Smalls…

● Several pistol shots

Cue: **Sides** Bye-bye, detective constable… er… thingy.

● Single pistol shot

Cue: **Amelia** Well, thank goodness that's over with…

ACT III

- Doorbell ring

Cue: **Smalls** I said "I think that's the doorbell now." I think that's the doorbell now.

- Single pistol shot

Cue: **Fickey** It was…

- Lights go out

Cue: **Sides** "Now, Nunnall, reveal…"

- Lights on again

Cue: After Fickey has counted to five.

Stage Set

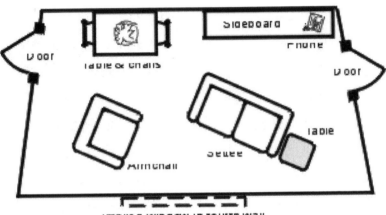

The above is a minimum set. Be creative: it's supposed to represent a room in a country manor, but be as surreal as you want!!!

Other plays by Ian Hornby - see www.scripts4theatre.com

Abanazar's Revenge	Jayne with a Y
Aladdin dot com	Late of This Address
'Allo, 'Allo, 'Allo, (Est There Any Body La)?	Mind Games
Are You Sure There's No Body There?	Murdered, Presumed Dead
Be Careful Who You Wish For	No, Minister
Boomerang	One Across
The Cat's Away	The Price to Pay
Cinderella	A Question of Innocence
Cold Blood	Remember Me
Conference Pairs	Robin Hood
The Dark Side of the Son	Shades of Blue
D I Why?	Situation Vacant
A Dish Served Cold	Tied Up at the Office
Do You Keep Stationery?	To Sleep, Perchance
Dream, Lover!	Voices
The Ex Factor	Wait Until the Ghost is Clear
An Eye for an Eye, Darling	Where There's a Will...
Hello, Is There Any Body There?	Whispers
Help! I'm a Celebrity Pantomime Dame; Get Me Out of Here!	Whose Line Was It, Anyway?
The Hex Factor	Why Won't They Believe Me?
Jack Up!	The Winter of Discontent

24195549R00045

Printed in Great Britain
by Amazon